Sarah Lawson was born in London, and brought up in rural Oxfordshire. She spent five years as a postal counsellor and leaflet writer for the *Woman's Own* magazine problem page, and now works as a freelance journalist, concentrating mainly on family issues. She lives in Berkshire with her partner and three children.

Overcoming Common Problems Series

For a full list of titles please contact
Sheldon Press, Marylebone Road, London NW1 4DU

Overcoming Common Problems Series

Overcoming Common Problems Series

Overcoming Common Problems

HELPING CHILDREN COPE
WITH BULLYING

Sarah Lawson

sheldon PRESS

First published in Great Britain in 1994
Sheldon Press, SPCK, Marylebone Road, London NW1 4DU

Second impression 1995

British Library Cataloguing-in-Publication Data
A catalogue record for this book is available from the British Library

ISBN 0–85969–683–9

Photoset by Deltatype Ltd, Ellesmere Port, Cheshire
Printed and bound in Great Britain by
Biddles Ltd, Guildford and King's Lynn

To Joe, Chris and Izzy

Contents

Acknowledgements

I couldn't have written this book without the unstinting help I received from many people. Angela Willans, recently retired as 'agony aunt' of *Woman's Own* magazine and my old boss, was one of these, and I am deeply grateful to her for giving me the benefit of her twenty-five years' experience. For the inspiration and guidance that really got this book off the ground, however, I have to thank Michele Elliott. With her tireless and enthusiastic campaigning on behalf of every child who is abused or bullied, Michele has probably done more than anyone else in this country to bring about change for the better.

Introduction

Emma's story

Emma had a normal, happy childhood until soon after her eleventh birthday, when she started secondary school. At first, things seemed to be going well. She made a few friends, and on the whole she was happy at her large comprehensive school. Sometime during the first year, however, things started to go wrong for Emma. The group she had been part of split up, and she was left on her own. Also in her year was a girl who had dominated her at primary school, and now that Emma didn't have the protection of her friends around her this girl started to pick on her again, and was soon joined by a handful of others.

Emma became unhappy at school, and told her parents that she wanted to leave and go to another local secondary school instead. The school were consulted, and promised action to stop the bullying, but in the event nothing was done and the bullying continued. Emma and her parents decided that a move was the best thing. In hindsight, they feel that it was the worst thing they could have done.

Emma was happy for her first few weeks at the new school, but then word got out that she had moved from her last school because of bullying. Before long the bullying had started again, but this time it was much worse and there were more children involved. At first it was mostly verbal abuse from other girls – slag, cow, bitch and so on. Soon it started to become more physical – the odd punch or kick, a push on the stairs resulting in a fall – and some boys joined in with the original group of girls.

Emma's parents approached the school as soon as it became apparent that a problem was developing. From the outset, they felt that the tendency was to blame Emma for what was happening. The bullying was referred to in correspondence and discussions as 'Emma's problem'. Among the solutions the school came up with was the suggestion that she should ask to see matron if the bullying got too bad, or that she could be set some work to do on her own. This felt to Emma, and looked to other children, like a punishment for being bullied. A visit from the educational psychologist was arranged, 'to help Emma look at the situations she finds herself in', and she was advised to change the way she responded to bullying.

Although the school did take some measures against the bullies, they seemed half-hearted, and this often made matters worse. One girl, a ringleader in the bullying, was told that she must stay inside during break times for a month as a punishment. Halfway through her first break time indoors, the supervising teacher went in and told her that she could come outside after all.

The situation in the school seemed to be out of control. On some occasions, teachers acknowledged that Emma had been bullied, but declined to tackle the culprits on the grounds that it would 'make matters worse for her'. Some teachers had trouble controlling their classes, and Emma would be struck from behind as she sat at her desk during lessons. Her possessions were taken and thrown around the room and one particular girl spat at her each time she passed.

Emma lived with this situation for two years, during which time her parents rang, wrote to or visited the school over fifty times. Their letters often went unanswered and their telephone calls unreturned. They were never told directly about the results of any investigations: sometimes a message was passed on to them via Emma, and sometimes they just heard on the grapevine that action had been take against a particular bully. Emma's physical and emotional health was deteriorating. Her mother had started a new job, and would come home to find that Emma hadn't been able to face going to school and had been at home on her own all day. She felt anxious and guilty, and the whole family suffered from the consequent stress. In desperation, Emma's parents contacted the police, who were very sympathetic, and told them that they would talk to the children involved and take action if an assault had been committed. Reluctantly, Emma's parents decided against this course of action, because they didn't want to put her through the stress of interviews and court proceedings.

Emma's parents did all they could to help her. They contacted ABC (the Anti-Bullying Campaign, a support group for parents of children who are being bullied at school) after reading an article about the group in a local newspaper, and with their help and support they approached individual teachers, the head and the school's board of governors, sending them all the information they could gather on the bullying and passing on leaflets from ABC and Kidscape (a charity devoted to the protection and safety of children), suggesting ways in which the school might bring the situation under control. The board of governors responded to their request for action by sending out a note to all parents saying that bullying would not be tolerated, but told Emma's parents they were confident that bullying was not a particular problem in their school, although Emma and other children knew that it was.

The final straw for both Emma and her parents came when, during an interview with her year head and class tutor in which Emma painfully recounted the incidents of bullying she had recorded in her diary, it became obvious that they simply didn't believe her. Her mother challenged the class tutor, who admitted that he thought she was making at least some of it up. Emma was devastated by this. As she said, 'They say you should tell, and when you do they don't believe you – what else can you do?' She became so depressed that, at fourteen, her parents removed her from school permanently.

A year later, Emma's confidence is still at rock-bottom. She doesn't go out with friends like most girls her age, and her education has ground to a halt. She would like to work in healthcare, perhaps as a nurse or care assistant, but she hasn't the confidence to go out and get the training she needs. As she says, 'If someone tells you you're bad often enough, you start to wonder whether it's true.'

Emma's story is far from unusual. During my five years as a member of the postal counselling team for the *Woman's Own* problem page I replied to as many as sixty letters each week from worried readers, and among them was a steady stream of problems involving bullying of one sort or another. Some were from anxious parents, some from the young victims themselves, some from children who had witnessed bullying and felt powerless to help. Perhaps the saddest of these bullying-related letters, however, came from adults who had been emotionally scarred for life by the bullying they had suffered as children; victimized by family, teachers or their peers, they had become trapped in a cycle of self-doubt, low expectation, failure and destructively unequal relationships.

It doesn't have to be like this. It would be unrealistic to suppose that we could ever stamp out bullying altogether – there will always be a few frightened, unhappy, inadequate or just plain obnoxious children who find that the power to hurt or intimidate others goes some way towards fulfilling their needs – but where parents, schools and children work together the effects of bullying can be minimized, sometimes even turned to the advantage of all concerned. Carol's story, below, is a good example of the way in which, with the support of parents and school, the bullied child can emerge from the experience with confidence and self-esteem intact, and better equipped to face the future.

Carol's story

Like Emma, Carol's problems started soon after her move to secondary school. She came from a primary school outside the area, and didn't know anyone at her new school. Within the first couple of weeks, a group of girls in her own year started to pick on her – and on anyone they saw with her. Although there were other girls in the class who might have made friends with her, they were discouraged by the prospect of being bullied themselves, and she was often on her own in the playground.

The bullying continued, and got worse. Other girls joined in, and she would be tripped up in corridors, her books and possessions were taken, and she would find nasty notes in her pockets and school bag. For a while she coped, but then she became depressed and anxious. Her parents guessed that something was wrong and asked her what was worrying her. Although she was reluctant to involve them at first, she eventually broke down and told them about the bullying, and her mother talked to her form tutor the following day.

Carol, her parents and her form tutor got together and it was decided that she should keep a diary of all the bullying incidents, when and where they took place, who was responsible and how they made her feel. Action was taken immediately to protect her from the worst of the bullying. Her form tutor reassured her that she could come and see him at any time she liked to talk about her worries, and she was given permission to go into the library at break and lunch times if she felt the need to get away. A general warning about bullying was given to the whole school in assembly, and Carol's form tutor and those of the other first year classes reinforced this individually.

The bullying didn't stop straight away, but some of the girls who had 'jumped on the bandwagon', and bullied Carol just because everyone else was, thought better of it. After a couple of weeks, it was obvious from Carol's diary who the persistent culprits were, and it was agreed that they would be summoned before the head of year. In a discussion between Carol, her parents, her year head and form tutor, Carol was asked if she would like to be present at the interview, and to her parents surprise, she decided that she would.

The three ringleaders were called into the year head's office and, in the presence of the year head and her form tutor, Carol recounted from her diaries all the incidents she had recorded over the past few weeks. Faced with Carol's record of her misery and humiliation, it was impossible for the bullies to claim that they hadn't done anything, were 'just teasing', or that Carol 'couldn't take a joke'. They were forced to admit to bullying, and were obviously shaken.

Given the choice of apologizing to Carol in person there and then or in writing the following day, they all chose to do so on the spot. All three were told they would be kept in at break and lunch times for three weeks, and warned that they would be suspended if they bullied again. Their parents were called in to see their year head, and told exactly what had happened, and what action had been taken.

Carol felt more confident than she had since the bullying started, perhaps even more confident than she had before. She had been listened to and believed by her parents and the school. Her distress had been recognized, and she had been involved in the subsequent investigation. She had been able to confront the bullies, who had acknowledged the wrong they had done and apologized. The blame for the bullying had been placed squarely where it belonged – on the bullies – and the whole of the first year was told by their form tutors that this was the way it had been, and always would be when bullying was uncovered.

This in itself would have been enough to ensure a positive outcome, but for Carol there was an added bonus. Soon after this incident, the local authority in Carol's area decided to undertake an anti-bullying initiative in its secondary schools. Carol's headteacher nominated her as an adviser to the committee responsible for the initiative, and extracts from her diary were used in an information pack distributed to all the schools in the area. As a result of prompt and appropriate action on the part of Carol's parents, the school and Carol herself, what could have been a damaging experience was turned to her advantage, and that of many more children in her school and others.

Emma, Carol and their parents are just two of the many families I spoke to while writing this book. In fact, once it was known that I was interested in bullying, practically everyone I met seemed to have a story to tell. I am very grateful to all of them, whether or not their stories eventually appeared in these pages. Their experiences formed the basis of this book, and none of the effort it cost them to talk about often very painful issues was wasted.

Why a book about bullying?

No one who has seen or experienced the results of bullying, both immediate and long term, could fail to take the problem seriously. Everyone whose opinion I sought – from the Department of Education and the Home Office down to individual teachers, youth workers and children themselves – agrees that bullying is a 'bad thing', and that 'something should be done about it'. Despite this general air of concern, this country still lacks a single coherent policy on just what that 'something' should be, and whose responsibility it is to get it done. Voluntary bodies like Kidscape and ABC have succeeded in bringing the problems of bullying to the forefront of public and media attention, but training for teachers, police officers and other professionals in the detection and prevention of bullying, and in understanding the needs of both victim and bully, is still thin on the ground, and uptake of what is available has been slow. Until anti-bullying provision in schools and in society as a whole catches up, it will often be up to parents to take the initiative when bullying is a problem.

All too often as parents, we learn to mistrust our instincts where our children are concerned. When problems arise, as they inevitably will from time to time, it is important not to lose sight of the fact that no one knows your child like you do, and no one cares as deeply as you about what happens to him. You will know, for example, when your child is really upset, and if your instinct is to protect, then that is exactly what you should do, even if friends, relatives, teachers and other 'experts' propose other courses of action, or no action at all. One of my aims in writing this book was to provide parents with the background, information and support they need to tackle bullying confidently and effectively, whatever form it takes and wherever it takes place.

Prevention

This book isn't just about picking up the pieces after a bullying incident, however. The conditions that encourage bullying and the factors that predispose children to involvement in it are largely avoidable, in the family, at school and in society. No book on coping with bullying would be complete without an exploration of the ways in which the problem can be avoided, or at least limited. As well as suggesting strategies to cope with existing bullying, a substantial part of this book is devoted to exploring some of the ways in which parents can help their children to develop the resilience, confidence and skills they need to avoid the bully/victim trap.

What can we do for the future?

Britain has one of the worst bullying problems in Europe. Everyone has their pet theory to explain the increase in the incidence and severity of bullying, but Kidscape founder Michele Elliott's explanation may come closest to the truth:

> Perhaps the root of the problem is the lack of direction in children's lives – a breakdown in parental/adult supervision and control. In the neighbourhood I grew up in, if you misbehaved outside your home – threw a stone at a cat or had a fight, for instance – someone who knew who you were would see you, and either tell your mum or grandmother, or take you to task there and then themselves. Now there is little sense of community for children, they are no longer accountable for their actions. They can misbehave in full view of a group of adults, and no one will make any attempt to stop them, because they don't feel any connection with them. This is giving children all the wrong messages.

If Michele is right, then there is something we can all do to help. If we can make our children feel that who they are and what they do is important, that their actions have consequences, and that we are all responsible for each other, we will be going a long way towards ending tacit acceptance of bullying behaviour. Teachers, police officers, youth workers and others can reinforce these beliefs, but only parents can make them a part of children's lives. If we really want to protect our children from bullying, we can and must do just that.

A note on gender

For readability's sake, I have opted to refer to 'he' or 'she' at random, rather than use 'him or her', 's/he', or any of the many other possible compromises. Girls and boys are equally likely to be both bully and victim, and everything in this book refers to both sexes, except where the context makes it obvious that this is not the case.

1

Defining the problem

The word 'bully' often conjures up a picture of a scruffy lad, big for his age, meting out clips round the ear to smaller boys in order to relieve them of their gobstoppers. In fact bullies come in all shapes and sizes and bullying itself is just as varied, so much so that defining what we mean when we say 'bullying' is by no means as straight-forward as it might seem at first sight. What does bullying mean? Does there have to be physical contact between bully and bullied, or can a purely verbal attack be classified as bullying? Docs a one-off incident count, or does the assault, whatever form it takes, have to take place on a weekly, or even a daily basis? What if the victim provokes the attack? What about 'teasing'? At the other end of the scale, can we really include violent attacks leading to serious injury, even death, in the same category as the pinching of dinner money? What about the bully? Does there have to be intent on his or her part to cause pain and humiliation or should we define bullying by its effects on the victim, rather than by what actually takes place between the children concerned?

Undoubtedly, the bully often intends to hurt and humiliate, but there are also many occasions, particularly amongst younger children, when the 'bully' has no conception of the damage she is doing – perhaps because teasing and baiting are a normal part of life in her family, or because she simply hasn't developed the ability to 'put oneself into someone else's shoes'. Whether or not we can properly define this as textbook bullying, it certainly feels like it to the victim.

The word 'victim' itself carries its own stereotype, of course. Perhaps we imagine a timid child, a bit of a runt, the sort of child we might have thought of as 'wet', or a 'mummy's boy' in our own schooldays. The sort of child, in fact, who is just asking to be bullied. This stereotype is no more accurate than the 'bully' tag. Bullying can and does happen to anyone. Often the 'victim' is simply in the wrong place at the wrong time – the child who walks home from school alone, for example, is an easier target for the bully than one who walks with friends or is collected by a parent, but the fact that he lives in a different street from his friends says absolutely nothing about him as a person. Unfortunately, the

English language doesn't offer a useable alternative to this emotive word. Although the dictionary definition of 'victim' is: 'One who suffers as a result of something', the alternatives offered by my thesaurus were 'dupe', 'fall guy', 'easy mark' and worse. Throughout this book, I use the word victim in its true sense: to describe the child who has suffered as the result of bullying.

Peter Stephenson and David Smith, two educational psychologists who have conducted research into bullying in Cleveland schools, define bullying as 'an interaction in which a more dominant individual or group intentionally causes distress to a less dominant individual or group'. The key feature of bullying, in their view, is the unequal nature of the interaction. The bully is stronger, either physically, socially or both, and will always win, the victim is weaker, and will always lose.

A comprehensive definition of bullying appears in a questionnaire based on the work of the Norwegian Dan Olweus, an internationally recognized authority in this field. This survey is now widely available in the UK as part of a package designed to assess the extent of the problem within individual schools. Its authors define bullying, for the benefit of the pupils who will answer its multiple-choice questions, as follows:

> We say a child is being bullied, or picked on, when another child, or a group of children, say nasty or unpleasant things to him or her. It is also bullying when a child is hit, kicked, threatened, locked inside a room, sent nasty notes, when no one ever talks to them and things like that. These things can happen frequently and it is difficult for the child being bullied to defend himself or herself. It is also bullying when a child is teased repeatedly in a nasty way. But it is not bullying when two children of about the same strength have the odd fight or quarrel.

Bullying in the UK

Much of what we know about patterns of bullying comes from the work of Dan Olweus. Since the early 1970s, the Norwegian government has taken the problem of bullying in schools very seriously, and has funded extensive research and an anti-bullying campaign. This contrasts starkly with the situation in the UK, where it has largely been left to voluntary bodies like Kidscape and ABC (The Anti-Bullying Campaign), to undertake research into the nature and frequency of bullying, and to institute training programmes in its recognition and prevention for those who work with children.

Much of the research that has been undertaken here has been part of broader studies into discipline and disruptive behaviour. The Department of Education has compiled no statistics on the subject, which they say would involve the reporting of every single incident of bullying, many of which are never seen by staff or recognized as such. As a result of concerns arising in the mid-eighties about classroom disruption, the Department of Education commissioned a survey into discipline in schools, resulting in the Elton report of 1989. Although it didn't look specifically at bullying, the report concluded that violence in schools was not a particular problem, as far as the perceptions of teachers were concerned – they saw minor misbehaviour in class as a far greater concern. This conclusion reflects the priorities of the teaching profession at the time, however, and might not be shared by the one-in-four children who are likely to have been involved in bullying. Neither does the Home Office class bullying as a separate category for statistical purposes, although the police may become involved in incidents of bullying where a criminal act has occurred.

Local Education Authorities have been slow to publish guidelines on bullying for the schools within their jurisdiction, but Nottinghamshire has taken a lead in this respect with the publication of its Action Checklist for Nottinghamshire schools. In the summary breakdown of research into bullying which accompanies the Checklist, the Members' panel that produced the document pinpoints the following commonly recurring themes:

- School break times are often the flashpoints for bullying, and a time of great anxiety for many children.
- The other major times when incidents occur are on the way to and from school and these too can be times of great stress for children, particularly as there is frequently no adult supervision at all.
- Both bullies and victims tend to perform poorly at school, and are less popular with teaching staff.
- Most bullying happens within class and year groups.
- Bullying between boys tends to be physical, whilst girls tend to rely more heavily on verbal and emotional bullying, although there is overlap.

- About one in four children are involved in bullying, either as bullies or victims.
- Cases of bullying generally last for twelve months or more.

These are useful pointers to the extent and nature of the problem, so let's look at some of the issues underlying them in more detail.

Where, when and how bullying takes place

The vast majority of bullying incidents take place at, or on the way to and from, school. Given our educational system, which gathers together large numbers of children of varying ages, concentrates them into one place, from which they are allowed no escape, and turns them loose together with minimal adult supervision for long periods every day, this shouldn't surprise us. Within the family, extended family or small community, with its mixture of age groups, there is a clearly defined and shared understanding of what is and is not acceptable behaviour. Away from this influence, children will make up their own rules with chaotic results, unless the school takes positive steps to establish its own sense of family and community. This is increasingly difficult in today's larger and larger schools, and not all achieve it.

Although school-related bullying generally takes place on the way to and from school, or during break times and lunch hours, this is by no means always the case. In some schools, verbal bullying and intimidation can continue into class time, and is occasionally condoned, and even encouraged by a teacher. Sometimes a teacher will appoint a victim by singling them out for special treatment. One little girl complained of bullying by other children in her class, so her mother approached her class teacher for help. The teacher reacted by standing the child up in front of the class and saying, 'Sophie's mother has complained to me because she thinks that Sophie is the only good child in this class, and all the rest of you are being nasty to her'. Of course, and as that teacher might have expected, the child was immediately marked out by other children in the class as a target for bullying.

Outside school, bullying can occur wherever children gather together – at or on the way to and from activities, between neighbours, in the informal gangs that tend to grow up in neighbourhoods. Bullying also takes place within families, and even between 'friends'. I remember well from my own childhood one

12

particular girl, the daughter of my mother's best friend, whom my mother was convinced was a special friend of mine. She was invited round frequently to play, and spent all the time that we were out of sight of adults criticizing my possessions, laughing at my efforts to play with her and telling me what a great time she would be having at home if she hadn't been dragged to my house. Oddly enough, I never told my mother about this, and to this day I don't believe that she had any idea what was going on.

Physical vs. mental/emotional bullying

Bullying breaks down into two main categories, although many bullies will use both:

- *Direct bullying*

  E.g., pushing, punching, name-calling, following home from school.

  Jason and Derek became well known at their comprehensive school for their bullying tactics. They would pick on boys a year or two younger than themselves whom they knew had school dinners, and start by calling them names in the playground or after school. If this yielded the results they wanted, over the course of a few days they would move on to pushing and shoving their victims and throwing their possessions around, and finally demanded that they hand over their dinner money each day in exchange for being left alone.

- *Indirect bullying*

  E.g., sending notes, hiding possessions, spreading nasty rumours.

  Ten-year-old Susan found the following note on her desk:

  Stinky Susan,
  You're the smelliest girl in the school. Why don't you wash? We all hate you, you big fat cow. Nobody wants to be your friend, so why don't you stop following us around at break. Perhaps you'll die, then we could all get some fresh air.

  From everyone

Although it is by no means always the case, research and observation have shown that there is a tendency for boys to be more direct in their approach to bullying while girls tend to use the more indirect approach.

Physical bullying can be terrifying and dangerous, but verbal bullying can be just as devastating to the victim, causing depression, misery and loss of self-esteem. It is also more difficult for parents and teachers to detect. If your child is beaten up at school, she will probably have bruises to show for it, even if she comes up with all sorts of plausible excuses for their presence, but the emotional distress caused by non-physical bullying can be hidden by the child or misinterpreted by the adults who could protect her. Most parents will remember the case of Katherine Bamber, the teenage girl who committed suicide in 1991 after suffering months of verbal bullying at school. Katharine's parents had approached her school a year before her death about the bullying to which she was being subjected, and believed that the problem had been sorted out. It was only when they read her diary after her death that they realized the bullying had continued, to the point where she couldn't face it any longer and took her own life.

Verbal/emotional bullying can, in fact, be potentially more damaging than the physical kind. In the words of one primary school head: 'The old adage about sticks and stones is complete nonsense. The worst form of bullying in terms of the distress it creates is often the girl who says simply and repeatedly "I won't be your friend".'

Julie, now in her thirties, still finds it distressing to recall the years of bullying and rejection she suffered at school:

I still don't really know what it was that made the other girls pick on me. I know that I was often depressed throughout most of my childhood, but I'm not sure whether I was depressed because I was bullied, or bullied because my depression made me an easy target.

I don't believe that I was ever bullied physically – pushed about and so on. I went to a private primary school, and that sort of thing would have been looked on as terribly common. What actually happened was much worse. The other children in my class – there were only about ten of us for most of my time at that school – just rejected me totally. In PE the team leaders were allowed to choose their teams, and I was always the last one left. I was almost never included in playground games, and if I was, it wasn't long before I did something that made everyone moan or laugh at me. The strange thing was that this sort of behaviour was seen by the staff at this school as completely acceptable – some teachers would even join in with the other children in making fun of my miserable attempts at netball and rounders. Although I did very well academically, passing both common entrance and 11 plus exams early, I left that school feeling a failure, and it has taken me many years since to convince myself of my own worth. I don't think that the feeling of inadequacy ever really goes away.

Single-sex vs. co-educational schools

Until recently, it was a generally accepted principle that boys bullied more than girls, due to their more naturally aggressive nature. Indeed, bullying has been seen by many as an inevitable, even a desirable part of a boy's development. In fact, as more recent research has revealed, girls are just as likely to bully, although the bullying often takes different forms and may not be identified by teachers or parents as such. Celestine Keise, in her study of bullying in two single-sex comprehensive schools in London, found that the same percentage of children – some two-thirds of the schools' pupils – had experienced bullying as either victim or bully at both the girls' and boys' schools.

So, is your child more or less likely to be bullied at a single-sex school? There hasn't been much research specifically into the effect of separating the sexes on the incidence and nature of bullying in schools, but what data there is indicates that a co-educational environment is safer for both boys and girls. A fascinating but limited survey by R. R. Dale, the results of which were published in 1971, confirms this trend, and goes some way towards explaining the reasons underlying it. The survey was based on the replies to a questionnaire of 620 women and 175 men, all students, each of whom had attended both a single-sex and a co-educational school. Almost half of the male students estimated that bullying was 'frequent' or 'very frequent' in their single-sex schools, while just over one fifth felt that the same was true of their mixed school. Of the women, around one in five thought that bullying was 'frequent' or 'very frequent' in their girls' school, and one in eighteen in their mixed school.

The students participating in the survey were encouraged to expand on their answers with comments, and many felt that the presence of the opposite sex had a moderating influence on the behaviour of both boys and girls – bullying behaviour was seen as downright unattractive, and both boys and girls cared enough about the opinions of others to want to avoid this.

Is bullying on the increase?

Perhaps the best guide to the scale of the problem in this country comes from the observations of those who work closely with children: teachers, social workers, psychologists and others. Teacher and educational psychologist Michele Elliott, founder of Kidscape, asserts that not only is bullying on the increase, but that the methods used by the bully have become more vicious – children are using knives and matches where previously they might have used fists and feet. This increase in the violence and severity of bullying seems to be moving down the age scale; in one incident, a seven-year-old boy was set on fire by other seven-year-olds. A further very disturbing development has been the incidence of violence to very young children by slightly older ones; most horrifying of these was the case of James Bulger, a two-year-old who disappeared from a Liverpool shopping precinct and was later found dead on a railway line. Two ten-year-old boys were later charged with his murder. This is bullying – the abuse of power over a weaker individual – carried to the extreme.

Bullying doesn't only happen between children, of course. Parents, teachers and other adults can and do bully children and other grown-ups. There are some areas of adult life where bullying has become institutionalized. New recruits to the Armed Services, for instance, are often subjected to a programme designed to break them down as individuals, so that they can be reformed as part of a unit. There have been well-publicized cases where those in charge of their training have apparently carried their task even beyond what their superiors expected of them, and severe psychological distress, serious injury and even the death of recruits has resulted. In some trades, it is still the practice for established employees to subject the new apprentice to a humiliating ritual – from sending him to the builder's merchant for 'a long weight' at one end of the scale, to stripping him and subjecting him to physical, often sexual assault at the other. Bullying of a less overt kind is also common amongst adults. Who has not encountered at least once the boss who belittles his employees at every opportunity, or makes conflicting demands on his staff that are impossible to fulfil? Who hasn't come across the car park attendant who obviously enjoys throwing his weight about, or been the newcomer in a group who talk animatedly amongst themselves, but ignore any attempt at conversation from the outsider?

Bullying, then, is not just something that happens at school, it touches everyone's life, adult or child. So why should we be concerned about it? Isn't it just a part of normal life, and isn't it a good thing for children to learn to cope with it early on?

Long-term effects of bullying

At every stage of life, bullying can have a profound and lasting effect on its victim. The fear and anticipation of the next incident can fill every waking moment, and spill over into nightmares, causing anxiety and depression without respite. Work and family relationships become impossible burdens, and the smallest of demands or setbacks can feel like the last straw to someone already pushed to the limit of their capacity to cope. In the short term, this can lead to withdrawal from family and social life, and failure at work or school. This in itself would be reason enough to take the problem very seriously, but the long-term effects of unchecked bullying, on both the victim and the bully, are also far-reaching and damaging. Tom, now a father in his forties, tells how bullying at school affected his outlook on life.

In those days, people didn't talk about bullying or do anything about it the way they do now, but everyone knew it went on all right. I can remember seeing the teachers lined up at the windows during break, looking at us kids beating each other up and slapping the little kids round the legs.

I wouldn't say it was all that vicious, but the bad thing about it was that there were some kids, including me, who always seemed to be on the receiving end, and never managed to get in any bullying of our own. It made you feel that you were cut out to be a victim, and I don't think I've ever really got over that approach to life. I don't have much confidence in myself, and I can never stand up to people when I should – I usually just let them walk all over me, and then hate myself for it afterwards.

To be honest, I don't think that the bullying would have had this effect if my parents had helped me over it in the beginning. I told them about it early on but, as I said, people just didn't reckon to do anything about it in those days, so they more or less said 'grin and bear it – don't be a sissy'. I did feel a sissy for not being able to avoid bullies, or give them a taste of their own medicine – I suppose I still feel like that, really.

Like Tom, the victims of bullying can be left with a lifelong lack of self-esteem and confidence. They may find it hard to believe that others will accept them, or that they can actually achieve anything worth while, and become shy, anxious or withdrawn. This outlook can attract further bullying, and the result of playground bullying can be an adult who is locked into the role of victim indefinitely.

It is not only the victim who suffers where bullying goes unchecked. One study has shown that, by the age of twenty-four, children who were persistent bullies at twelve are twice as likely as others to have a criminal conviction, and four times more likely to become multiple offenders. If they are not helped, they will carry their attitudes with them into adult life, marriage and parenthood, and are more likely than the general population to experience marital breakdown and child-care problems, alcohol abuse, employment problems and psychiatric disorder, as well as continued aggressive behaviour. Bullying also affects the bystander. In a survey conducted by Kidscape, it was found that children who had witnessed incidents of bullying without being involved remained upset and anxious about what they had seen, feeling guilty for not intervening and afraid that they might become the next victim.

So, bullying doesn't 'toughen children up for life', it isn't a normal, harmless childhood prank; it is damaging and painful for all concerned, and ultimately for the whole of our society. So what can we do to protect our children and others? First, we need to understand the factors that can lead a child to become a bully – or a victim.

2

What makes a victim/bully

The labels 'victim' and 'bully' can be misleading. In many cases, the factors that lead a child to bully and to become the victim of bullying are the same – indeed, the same child may simultaneously play the role of both victim and bully, or move from one to the other at various times during his childhood or school life. Until recently, it was more or less universally accepted that older children bullied younger children, who got their turn to bully younger children as they progressed up the age scale. In a study of 783 children aged between 7 and 13 years attending 4 state schools in Dublin, it was found that only about a third of those children identified as bullies had never themselves been the victim of bullying, and less than half of the children identified as victims had never bullied others. Researchers have observed that persistent bullies often think of themselves as victims, feeling that it is they who are constantly and unfairly picked on by others.

The bully

Bullies can be classified broadly into three categories, each with different problems and motivations, and each needing a distinctly different form of help from parents and teachers to overcome her difficulties – and she can be helped. Even where things have gone wrong in a child's formative years to the extent that she becomes a persistent bully, with professional guidance, she and her family can get back on the right track, and her behaviour can be changed permanently.

The aggressive bully

This is the bully as we all know and recognize him – confident, brash, tough, and insensitive to the feelings of others. He will probably have plenty of friends and be popular with his peers. He likes to throw his weight about, and to get what he wants. He will not readily submit to authority, and will be difficult for teachers and other adults to handle. He may be, or become, involved in other forms of anti-social behaviour such as stealing or vandalism.

The aggressive bully needs to learn to control his aggression, and to be aware of and value the needs and feelings of others. These things are best learned by example within the family (see chapter 5: A good start), but if this influence has been absent or failed, the aggressive bully needs to be shown clearly that there are limits beyond which his bullying behaviour will not be accepted or tolerated. Both at school and at home, he needs to be supervised closely, and to be given a set of rules of behaviour which he is expected to stick to without exception, with clearly understood penalties for transgression. These rules should, however, be realistic, and good behaviour should be praised and rewarded just as assiduously as bad behaviour is condemned and punished.

The anxious bully

This child is likely to be both bully and victim. She is characterized by low self-esteem, anxiety and emotional instability. Anxious bullies are likely to be unpopular with other children, and to do badly at school. The anxious bully feels a failure, and bullying others may give her a feeling of power and success that she can't get in other ways; it also brings her the attention she craves, even though that attention may come in the form of anger and punishment. Behaving badly may be a way of living up to her negative self-image: she feels like a bad person, so she behaves like one.

This child needs help to see herself differently. The measures outlined in chapter 4 for building confidence will help, but a child who has become locked into this pattern of behaviour may well need professional help and support, as well as the co-operation of the school in overcoming her feelings of inadequacy and failure. It isn't easy to admit that your child has problems that you can't handle alone, but if you feel that your child's behavioural problems are prompted by anxiety and low self-esteem it is important to remember that she can be helped, and to pull out all the stops to get the help she needs. A good first step is to ask your GP to refer you to the local Child Psychiatry Service, Child Guidance Clinic, or its equivalent. If your GP seems reluctant to refer you, you can refer yourself. Look in your local telephone directory under the name of your local authority for details of the Child Guidance Clinic for your area.

The passive bully

This child is the 'hanger-on' in the bullying gang. He doesn't particularly want to bully other children himself, but he does want to be part of the group, and is willing to do things he knows aren't right, partly in order to gain acceptance and partly because he doesn't feel individually responsible for his actions. This propensity of human beings in general to do things as part of a group that they would not consider doing as individuals has been responsible for some of the most shameful episodes in history, and applies as much to children as to adults, perhaps even more. The passive bully may also feel that it is safer to be part of the gang than to risk being one of their victims. He is likely to understand the harm that is being inflicted on the victim, and to feel guilty about it afterwards.

Since this child has no real need or desire of his own to bully others, he will stop if the drawbacks to him outweigh the advantages. In an environment where bullying is seen as totally unacceptable, and where strong and consistent measures are taken against the bully on every occasion, he will probably never start.

If your child falls into this category, you can probably best help him by reinforcing his own feeling that what he is doing is very wrong, and making him understand that the pain he has caused is his responsibility, and his alone, even if he was in a group of children who were all doing the same thing.

Temporary bullies

Not all children who bully do so as the result of long-term problems arising from their upbringing or their family life. Sometimes an upsetting event like moving house, a parent's illness or the arrival of a new baby can give rise to aggressive behaviour. If handled carefully, this temporary bullying will usually tail off when the turbulent emotions that triggered it have settled down.

Some children turn to bullying because they have little alternative. In a school where bullying flourishes, it may be a case of 'bully or be bullied'. If the school seems unable or unwilling to tackle the problem effectively, the only answer may be a change of school.

Even where there is an obvious cause for bullying behaviour, though, it is important that parents and teachers make it clear that this is not the right way to handle problems – if it proves a good way of getting what she wants, the temporary bully may be tempted to continue after the original cause has ceased to be a factor.

If your child bullies

Most parents who are told that their child has been involved in bullying are taken completely by surprise. As any teacher will tell you, though, children can be completely different away from the influence of their family. However much you don't want to believe that your child has bullied another, don't dismiss the idea out of hand. The way in which you handle the matter is important to your child, and could make the difference between him becoming a persistent bully or moving on to more mature ways of handling problems and frustrations.

In all cases, make it clear that you take any incidence of bullying very seriously indeed. A formal family discussion can help here, though it shouldn't degenerate into a brow-beating session. Give the child a chance to state his case too.

The bully should never be allowed to escape the consequences of his actions, but he does need help to get back on the right road if he is to avoid problems in the future. The moral dilemma here is how much weight should be given to helping the bully, possibly at the expense of his victims, and it may be that only his removal from the school will satisfy the needs of those he has bullied, even if it is not the best answer for the bully himself.

The victim

As we have seen, the victim and the bully may be one and the same person. Where the victim of bullying does not fall into the category of bully/victim, bullying is often a matter of chance – the victim is simply in the wrong place at the wrong time, and the bully will go on to bully another child if this victim is removed. Some authorities have made an attempt to categorize the victims of bullying, broadly dividing them into two types.

The passive victim

This quiet, timid child looks an invitingly easy victim to bully. She is anxious and lacking in self-esteem, failing to defend herself and crumpling satisfyingly under the bully's taunts, threats or blows.

The provocative victim

The provocative victim provokes bullying by outrageous behaviour. She is hot-tempered, creating situations where conflict arises easily, and fights back in the face of teasing and bullying, perhaps escalating the incident.

There are dangers, however, in attempting to categorize the victims of bullying at all. Unfortunately, many schools still tend to look on all children who are bullied as somehow provoking the bully's behaviour, even though those teachers who are quite happy to accept this view would probably be horrified at the suggestion that the attractively dressed woman who became the victim of a rape was 'asking for it' – a very similar proposition.

Labelling some children 'natural victims' serves simply to deflect the guilt and responsibility for bullying away from the bully and on to the victim. There is no doubt that some children are better equipped than others to withstand the bully's attacks – self-confidence, a sense of humour and the ability to take life as it comes all help, and we will see in chapter 5 how we can help our children to achieve these qualities – but it would be wrong to see the child who becomes the bully's victim as somehow deficient or at fault. This compounds the damage done to the victim, offends against children's natural sense of justice and fairness, and can amount to an excuse for doing nothing to change the conditions in which bullying flourishes.

Nevertheless, from the bully's point of view, some children make more satisfactory victims than others. Although we cannot predict with any certainty which individual child will become the victim of bullying, we can identify factors that put a child at higher than average risk of being bullied. We all have 'crumple buttons' – topics or issues about which we are particularly sensitive, and which provide a direct route to our emotions and insecurities. For some of us it is a physical feature – a big bottom or a small bust – for others the crumple factor is less easily identified, perhaps the anxiety that there is something inherently unlovable about us, or a fear of confrontation. The bully is looking for someone whose crumple buttons he can easily find and push, producing an immediate and intense response and giving him a degree of power over his victim. This button pushing can be set up within the family by parents or other children, or may be made easier for the bully by some trait that sets the victim apart from other children.

Risk factors

● *Poor self-image*

Children who have doubts about themselves will be easy prey for the bully, who will soon learn to concentrate on those areas his victim feels most uncertain and anxious about. Feeling good about yourself starts within the family, and all children need at least enough positive input from parents to balance the negative side of their relationship – praise for what they do right as well as criticism for what they do wrong. Some parents find this hard to give, especially if they were made to feel worthless by their own parents.

● *Bullying at home*

There is a fine line between firmness and bullying. However hard we try, all parents overstep this line occasionally, and it is all too easy to give your child the impression that bullying is OK as long as you are in a position of authority over your victim – i.e., he is younger, smaller or a junior member of your own family or group. Faced with constant nagging, varying expectations and unreasonable demands, a child will soon learn to ignore them if at all possible, and a vicious circle can develop in which the parent has to exert more and more pressure in order to get any response. When browbeating, yelling and threats are no longer effective, the desperate parent may resort to blows in an attempt to get their child to obey. This child will come to see bullying as the way to get things done, and tend both to respond to the bullying approach and to use the same tactics on others. It can sometimes be hard to avoid bullying your child, particularly if you have been brought up that way yourself. Chapter 5 looks at some common situations in which bullying between parent and child can occur, and offers alternative strategies for dealing with them constructively.

● *Bullied by siblings*

Brothers and sisters will tease and bully one another from time to time. As we will see in chapter 5, family teasing and arguments can help to prepare children for situations they will encounter outside the home, and parents need not intervene unless the argument is very unequal, one child is obviously becoming very upset, or physical violence takes over. On the whole, children will base the way they treat each other on the way they see their parents behave: if parents bully each other and their children, the children will, in turn, tend to bully amongst themselves, and woe betide the one who ends up at the bottom of the heap.

Occasionally bullying between brothers and sisters gets out of hand, and a child becomes the victim of sustained abuse. Cherry was one such victim. Her earliest memories are of her older brother pushing her around and taking her toys when she was about four, and he was seven. He was a sickly child, with chronic asthma and chest problems, and had always been a worry to his family. Cherry's parents had an unequal relationship. Her father was an only child, waited on hand and foot by his mother until he left home to marry, and demanded the same degree of attention from his wife. She was often depressed, and had little love or support left to give Cherry after looking after her demanding husband and sickly son.

Cherry came to feel that her needs and wants were unimportant, and would never be fulfilled. When her brother pushed her around and took things from her, she reacted by withdrawing into herself, never fighting back or asking for help from her parents. Her brother tended to treat her very much as he saw his father treat his mother, and would send her to fetch and carry things for him, never thanking her for doing so, and constantly criticizing her efforts to please him. As time went on, his demands on her changed, and he began to abuse her sexually. This went on until she was nearly sixteen years old, when she finally told a teacher what was happening, whereupon Cherry was removed from her home by Social Services and lodged with a series of friends. Her brother stayed with his parents. Cherry fell into a series of disastrous relationships with demanding and dominating men, puncutated by depression and suicide attempts. Now in her late twenties, she is just beginning to understand that what happened was not her fault, but has a long way to go before she can cope with life without considerable support.

Cherry's was an extreme case. In most families, bullying between siblings stops short of severe physical or sexual abuse, but it is important that parents realize the damage that can be done by persistent bullying within the family, even when it seems relatively harmless. The older sister who constantly knocks your attempts to keep up with her, the brother who constantly tells you how stupid you are, can set up just the kind of 'crumple buttons' that the bully looks for in a potential victim.

The 'different' child

● *Racial differences*

Racial bullying is a severe problem in some schools. Limited surveys in multiracial schools, both primary and secondary, suggest that racial name-calling is pretty common, with around one third or more of pupils reporting that they had been teased about their colour. Black children had suffered in this way more often than white, and Asian children most of all. It is probably true to say that, where bullying is a problem within a school, race will be one of the factors in deciding which children will become victims. This may sometimes be because of true racial prejudice on the part of the bullies, but more often happens because, in an environment where bullying is seen as acceptable or unavoidable, race is a convenient peg to hang it on – a factor which picks out an easily identifiable person or group as 'fair game' for the bully.

Racial bullying is not confined to schools, and any child who is in a racial minority within a group or area may be subjected to racial bullying. The best defence your child can have is to be prepared for racial abuse (see chapter 4 for ideas on how you can help). Where racial abuse or bullying is taking place at school, this is a matter for your child's form tutor, year head, headteacher and ultimately the school governors (see chapter 7).

● *Special needs or physical handicap*

Children with special needs who are attending a normal school can start with a disadvantage as far as bullying is concerned: their needs can make them obviously different from their classmates, and in a school where bullying flourishes these differences may be seized upon by other children and turned into taunts and intimidation. It need not be this way, and most schools which are happy to integrate children with special needs into their normal classes will have devoted considerable thought to the problems that might arise, and forestalled them by preparing the children for the presence of a child whose needs, strengths and abilities are different from their own. Where the situation is handled well, the integration of special needs children with their able-bodied peers can bring great benefits for all concerned.

Problems are more likely to arise where a child with unrecognized special needs has struggled to compete with other children at school. Often, frustration and unhappiness will lead such a child to behave badly at school and at home, and by the time the problem is identified she may already be seen by teachers, classmates and even parents as a misfit. Such a child is likely to suffer severe damage to her confidence and self-esteem, bringing with it an increased risk of involvement in bullying. The principals and staff of special schools will usually be well aware that children who come to them may already have an established bully/victim problem, and take special measures to control the problem within their school. At Holyport Manor School in Berkshire, a large residential and day school catering for children with a broad range of special needs from mental and physical handicap to learning and behaviour difficulties, headteacher Tony Whittard has instigated a programme of once-a-week individual counselling sessions for all pupils, giving them the opportunity to talk about any problems they are encountering within the school or outside. The staff/pupil ratio in special schools makes this sort of provision, undreamed of in other state schools, a possibility.

Be prepared

If your child looks, sounds or behaves differently from others, because of race or culture or as a result of a physical peculiarity like a birthmark, a speech defect or a mental or physical disability, you can be pretty sure that someone, somewhere, will eventually use that difference to taunt her. The very best defence your child can have is to be prepared in advance for everything that the bully might throw at her (see chapter 4).

Not all bullying is so predictable, however; often the victim just happens to be in the wrong place at the wrong time, and whether or not the bullying continues may depend largely on how she reacts. Despite all that we know about the nature of bullying and the factors that predispose a child to become a bully or victim, it really is not possible to predict with any certainty whether an individual child will be affected. So how will you know if it happens to your child? In the next chapter, we will look at the tell-tale signs of bullying that every parent should be aware of.

3

Is my child being bullied?

It is unlikely that your child will tell you if he is being bullied. Many bullies will warn their victims not to tell 'or it will get worse for you', and the embarrassment of the situation being made public to their classmates, and perhaps the whole school, sometimes outweighs the misery of the bullying itself. Secondary-school children, who are engaged in the process of becoming independent from their parents, may find it particularly hard to admit to them that they can't handle the situation on their own. The sort of anxiety that results from bullying can't be completely hidden, though, and most parents will be well aware that something has gone wrong in their child's life, even though there may be no obvious clues that bullying is at the root of the problem.

As Valerie Besag, one of the UK's leading authorities on bullying, has written in *Bullying: a practical handbook for schools*: 'Given that many bullied children find it difficult to approach their parents for help, the optimum situation must be that all parents are alerted to the possibility of bullying occurring, be made aware of the warning signs, and be encouraged to approach the school should they suspect anything untoward.'

Tom was in his first term at secondary school when his mother started to realize that something was worrying him.

He is normally quite a quiet, placid boy, but he started to fly into apparently uncontrollable rages over really trivial things – a disagreement with his sister over which TV programme to watch, for instance, or a request to tidy away his things from the living room. He would burst into tears at the slightest suggestion of criticism from anyone in the family, and shut himself in his room. I asked him repeatedly if there was anything worrying him, but he refused to talk to me at all.

One day, after a particularly nasty row, I went to his room to talk to him. He flew into a rage, screaming that no one cared about him, picked up a shoe and flung it at his bedroom window, smashing it. I think he frightened himself, and he certainly frightened me – I realized then that something had to be done.

Tom still wouldn't talk to his mother, so she enlisted the help of his thirteen-year-old sister, Sam, who was also very worried about him. Sam agreed to talk to Tom, and try to find out what was wrong.

I was so worried that I did something I would never dream of doing under any other circumstances – I eavesdropped on their conversation. Sam handled things wonderfully, and Tom eventually told her that he was being bullied in the playground at school by a group of boys. The bullying was more verbal than physical, but he said some things that really frightened me – that he felt no one cared about him and he didn't want to go on living. He made her promise not to tell me about the bullying, because he was afraid I would go to the school and make things worse for him. She did tell me in a roundabout way – she realized how important it was for him to get help – but of course I already knew the full story.

Tom's mother approached his year head, and the problem was sorted out without Tom knowing that she had been involved at all. If it had not been for the help of his older sister, however, the bullying might have continued, unrecognized by parents or school.

Behaviour problems indicating bullying

Tom clearly felt victimized and afraid, and these feelings spilled over into his relationships with his family, causing the violent rows and aggressive behaviour that worried his mother so much. Bullying can affect the victim in many ways, however, and the behaviour problems that result are not always so clearly linked to the cause. Any of the following may indicate that a child is being bullied, although there may be other causes.

● *Withdrawal*

The bullied child may be quiet and withdrawn, to the point of appearing sullen. He may find it difficult to do anything positive at all, and spend most of his time at home apparently daydreaming or just doing nothing. The unhappy child may seek an escape to a fantasy world by watching television or playing computer games, where he can leave behind his doubts about his own ability to cope, and be someone else for a while. Family outings, out-of-school activities and visits to friends, once a source of pleasure, may become an ordeal, and the child may prefer to stay at home alone.

● *Becoming difficult and argumentative*

The bullied child may have an exaggerated awareness of any unfairness or favouritism within the family, and feel victimized and put upon in circumstances where this is clearly not the case. She may resent any minor criticism or demand on her time out of all proportion to the event – a request to tidy her room, for instance, may provoke a flood of tears and protests of 'You're always going on at me – you never tell anyone else to tidy their room!', although this is patently untrue.

Underlying these responses is the feeling that 'everyone's picking on me!'

● *Aggressive behaviour*

All the pent-up anger and frustration felt by the bullied child has to go somewhere, and he may 'act out' his feelings by behaving aggressively towards brothers and sisters, or children outside the family. He may pick fights, become overly possessive of toys or food, or overreact to the normal, everyday arguments that are an inevitable part of family life. In an attempt to re-establish his damaged self-esteem and confidence, the victim may become a bully himself.

● *Fear of going to school*

If the bullying is taking place at school, or on the way there, the bullied child may refuse to go, ask repeatedly to be driven rather than walk or catch the bus, or develop frequent mystery illnesses that necessitate staying at home. Once at school, she may report to sick bay with headaches or stomach upsets, asking to be sent home. Some children will develop full-blown school phobia, where the prospect of going to school is so terrifying that the child will beg, plead, threaten and even become physically ill if parents insist she goes.

● *Schoolwork problems*

Children who are being bullied at school may spend all their time there in a state of fear and apprehension, anticipating the next attack. It really isn't possible to concentrate or learn effectively under these circumstances, and not surprisingly their schoolwork may suffer. They may fail to hand in homework because their books have been taken, but prefer to say that they left it at home and take the consequences themselves rather than report the bully.

● *Missing possessions*

School books may be damaged or lost, dinner money and other possessions may go missing, and your child may come home starving, having had sandwiches or dinner money stolen. Sometimes the victim of bullying will try to placate the bully with presents of toys, sweets or money. He may offer implausible excuses for loss or damage to his property: 'I lent them to a friend, I can't remember his name', 'I dropped it on the way to school and a car ran over it'.

● *Nightmares and disturbed sleep*

The bullied child may have nightmares, perhaps calling out 'no, don't', or 'leave me alone'. She may be obviously very tired, but delay bedtime as long as possible, knowing that her fears will catch up with her while her guard is down. Disturbed sleep will leave her tired in the morning, and it will be quite an effort to get her off to school on time, particularly as school may be the last place she wants to be.

● *Bed-wetting*

Bed-wetting is a sure sign of anxiety, and bullying is always worth considering as a possible cause. Michele Elliott recalls that in her early days as a child psychologist she would frequently see children who wet the bed, and would advise the parents to use a bed-wetting alarm to change the child's behaviour. She soon realized that this approach did nothing to address the cause of the problem. 'Now I would say – this child is clearly anxious about something, let's find out what it is!'

● *Stealing*

The child who is the victim of a 'protection racket' – 'Give us at least 50p every day or we'll beat you up on your way home' – may have to steal to satisfy the bully's demands. He may become involved in criminal activity, such as shoplifting, because of threats from other children, or the fear of rejection by the group if he doesn't. Children may also steal because they feel unloved, uncared for and misunderstood, and money or possessions taken from parents become a substitute for the love, attention and security they crave.

● *Injuries*

A child who is being bullied physically may have obvious bruises which she will try to explain away. Injuries incurred in school time and reported to staff, in a PE lesson for instance, will be recorded in the school accident book, along with their cause and any treatment given, so it is possible to ask the school to check up on your child's explanations if you suspect that suspiciously frequent injuries may have been inflicted by another child at or outside school.

● *Low self-esteem*

The victim of verbal bullying may try desperately to change the attributes that the bullies have picked upon for ridicule, asking for a different style of shoes or clothing, or becoming painfully self-conscious about some aspect of his appearance. Some children deliberately fail in their schoolwork after being called 'teacher's pet', others resort to obsessive washing after being called 'smelly' or 'dirty'.

The mother of one fourteen-year-old girl became anxious when her daughter refused to eat properly:

> She was literally starving herself all day – she would skip breakfast, the sandwiches I made her for lunch would be untouched in her lunch box when she got home, and she would find some excuse not to eat what the rest of the family had for an evening meal. She gradually ate less and less until she was living on peanut butter, which she ate by the spoonful, and baked potatoes – the only thing she would eat whenever we had a family meal. We tried to reassure her that she didn't need to lose weight, but she either insisted that she did or pretended that she just wasn't hungry that day. It turned out that one particular girl at school had been picking on her, calling her 'fatty' and that sort of thing – she wasn't overweight, although she does have a naturally fairly heavy build.

Fortunately, Annie's class tutor became aware of the situation, and the bully was moved to a different class. Annie's eating gradually returned to normal.

● *Regression*

An unhappy or frightened child may revert to earlier patterns of behaviour, taking several steps backward in her development. Some will become more dependent, and start clinging to mum again. Younger children may literally wet themselves during the day with anxiety, while older children may wet the bed. Thumb-sucking, nail-biting, overeating, stammering and habits like chewing clothing or bedding are all signs of anxiety which may be caused or contributed to by bullying.

● *Depression*

Children, like adults, can and do become truly depressed. Lethargy, tearfulness, difficulty in concentrating, loss of appetite or compulsive eating and a tendency to overreact to the slightest setback are all symptoms of depression. *Depression, with or without threats of suicide should always be taken seriously. The depressed or suicidal child needs urgent help – forcing him to school will only make matters worse.*

Any or all of the above could indicate that your child is being bullied, but most of them could be caused by a variety of other worries, so how will you know if bullying is at the root of your child's problems? First, and most importantly, you can encourage your child to talk to you about what is worrying her. This isn't easy at the best of times, and can become more difficult as children get older. Ideally, you will have established a relationship of open communication with your child long before a crisis arises; you can do this simply by showing an interest in her activities and opinions on a day-to-day basis, and by sharing your own activities and opinions with her. It sounds easy and obvious, but often we are too busy and preoccupied to talk to our children about what is important to them, and this makes it all the harder to do so when it really matters. Bullying is an emotive issue, laden for both parent and child with fears of inadequacy, rejection and failure. This can make it a difficult and embarrassing topic of conversation for both, particularly where older children are concerned. Parents who have been bullied themselves may be especially panic-stricken at the thought of their children suffering as they did, and feel extremely uncomfortable about discussing bullying with them, even in a general context. Children are extraordinarily sensitive to these sorts of feelings, and will quickly learn that bullying-related worries are off limits as far as their parents are concerned. Similarly, parents who have experienced bullying may be quick to interpret normal disagreements and fallings-out between children as bullying, and communicate their concern to their child.

Parental concern about bullying is justified and valuable. Knowing the dangers and understanding what bullying feels like can help you to make the right decisions when choosing your child's schools and activities, encouraging friendships and interpreting his reactions. If your concern makes it difficult to talk to your child in a supportive way about his own experiences, though, it is worth giving some thought to what it is about the subject of bullying that upsets you so much, and trying to separate your own fears from your child's experiences. Talking to someone often helps.

If you feel that something is wrong, but are finding it difficult to talk to your child, here are some strategies that may make it easier for you to raise the subject, and help her to talk about her worries:

- *Getting the questions right*

One of the problems may be that you are asking the wrong questions. Many younger and even some older children are really not sure what bullying is, and unless the issue has been discussed at school, home or both, they may not realize that they are being bullied at all, even though they are very upset and anxious about what is happening. Asking 'Are you being bullied?', therefore, may not elicit any useful response. More general questions about who they played with at school, what they did and how they felt about it are more likely to tell you what you need to know.

- *I didn't expect the Spanish Inquisition*

It's very hard to accept that your own child doesn't want to confide in you, especially when you are sure that you could sort out whatever's worrying her *if only she'd tell you what it is*! Difficult though it is to avoid it, the 'you're going to sit here until you've told me what's wrong' approach just doesn't get results, and will make it even harder for your child to confide in you. Try to keep things casual, and be prepared to leave it for another time if your first attempt doesn't succeed.

● *'When I was a girl . . .'*

Telling your child stories about real or imaginary things that happened to you during your own childhood can show that you are capable of understanding his problems, and open the way for him to say, 'and what did you do about it?', or even, 'that happened to me too!' You can make your ploy less obvious by leading into your story in a casual way, perhaps inventing a phone call from an old school friend that reminded you of your schooldays. Your child may well see straight through all this, of course, but still welcome the opportunity to talk about what is worrying him without committing himself to revealing more of his feelings than he can handle.

● *Play*

Therapists and social workers often use play to help younger children talk about painful or difficult experiences. Dolls or play-people can stand in for real characters, and children will often reveal in play the situations that are preying on their minds in real life. Simply watching your child play alone or with others may be enough to give an indication of what is going on, but if you want to lead the play yourself, it is best to be fairly casual about the whole thing; suggest that you make a playgroup for the toys, for instance: 'This doll could be Sally, this could be Mrs Jenks – who will this one be? Which one is you?' If bullying behaviour appears in your child's play, it is a pretty fair bet that she has seen or experienced it in real life.

Drawing or painting can also give children the means to express worries they find it difficult to talk about, and this in itself can be a therapeutic experience for the bullied child. Apart from the benefit to the child of expressing his feelings in this way, looking at your child's work may give you vital clues as to what's worrying him. The meaning of his pictures may not be immediately obvious, but symbols of aggression or threat may give the game away: perhaps he draws himself as a tiny figure amongst larger figures with angry faces, or creates terrifying monsters with dripping fangs. The child whose confidence is at a low ebb may draw a self-portrait as he sees himself: unhappy, ugly, insignificant.

If your child can't or won't tell you what's going on, you may have to resort to detective work to get to the root of the problem:

● *Asking other children*

If your child is being bullied at school, other children will certainly know about it. Asking the parents of her friends and classmates to find out if their child is aware of any problem your child is having at school can be very productive, although they will have to be tactful in their questioning if they are to avoid giving the game away. Sometimes an older brother or sister at the same school, or the brother or sister of a friend, will be able to find out what is going on.

● *Approaching a group leader or teacher*

If you suspect your child is being bullied at school or at an out-of-school activity, a teacher or group leader may be able to shed some light on the situation. Even if they haven't noticed anything wrong, ask them to keep an eye on the situation, and they may be able to report back to you later with helpful information.

● *Surveillance*

Try arriving to pick your child up from school a little earlier than usual: does he hang around with friends for a while, or does he shoot out of the cloakrooms as quickly as possible to avoid other children? What happens if you drop him off early for school? Does he go off into the playground happily and meet friends, or does he hover on the edges, near to the protection of other adults? Why not pass the school at break or lunch time and have a look at what's going on in the playground? Of course, your child would probably be horrified and embarrassed to find that you were spying on him, and this is probably only worth doing if you think you can go unnoticed.

Trust between parent and child is important, and I hope that most parents wouldn't ordinarily consider eavesdropping on their child's conversations, reading their private diaries or spying on their activities. The suffering and damage that can be inflicted on a bullied child is so great, however, that worried parents may feel that, in this case, the end justifies the means. Each family will have to make an individual choice when it comes to the tactics they use to arrive at the truth in a situation where their child is obviously disturbed and bullying may be implicated.

Don't forget that a child doesn't have to be the victim of bullying to be worried about it. Witnessing bullying incidents without involvement, or even being part of a group which is bullying other children, even if she is not taking an active part herself, can cause great anxiety. This child, too, will need the help of her parents to understand the full implications of what is going on, and to take action to end the bullying.

Parents' reactions

So, you've established at last that bullying is at the root of your child's problems. How do you feel? Parents' reactions to the news that their child is being bullied can be profound, and sometimes surprising, as Daniel's mother found.

I had suspected that Daniel was being bullied at school for some time, but nothing prepared me for my reaction when my suspicions were confirmed. I was in a state of total turmoil, overwhelmed by the instinct to protect my child at all costs, but not knowing how on earth I was going to achieve this. My first impulse was to find out which children had been bullying him and go after them myself – I don't know what I would have done if I had been faced with those children at that moment – but I soon realized that this would be counterproductive in the long run, even if it made me feel better in the short term.

I found out about the bullying over the weekend, from a neighbour who had been told about it by her daughter, and the hardest thing was sending Daniel off to school on Monday morning. I arranged to see his teacher the same day, but by the time I got to the school I was in tears. Fortunately, she was very sympathetic – mostly, I think, because she had a son of about the same age who was unhappy at school, though for different reasons. She seemed to understand how upset I was.

Parenthood is riddled with doubt and guilt, and a crisis brings these feelings to a head. Should we have done things differently? Have we, despite our best intentions, ruined our child's life by bungling his upbringing? Will we ever be able to stop worrying?

The first instinct of most parents faced with an unhappy and frightened child is to protect that child from the source of their anxiety at all costs. Parents who have to take their children to hospital for unpleasant tests or treatment often say they had to remind themselves constantly that the staff carrying out the procedures were, in fact, doing so for the child's benefit   their instinct being to hit the doctor, grab the child and run. Bullying can arouse the same sort of feelings: an overwhelming desire to deal with the bullies, or to shield your child by keeping her away from school. These instinctive reactions, however, sometimes conflict with the advice we may receive from relatives, friends, teachers or other 'experts'. 'Don't keep her off school – if you give in to her now, she'll think she can always get away with it', 'She's got to learn to stand on her own two feet', 'You'll turn him into a mummy's boy'.

Sadly, the feelings that bullying arouses in parents are sometimes so distressing that they make their child the focus of their anger and guilt. Fathers particularly may find it hard to accept that this could have happened to their son. Why didn't he stand up for himself? How will he cope with life if he can't cope with a bit of playground teasing? How could a son of mine get into this situation? These feelings are understandable, but completely unhelpful to the child who, now more than ever, desperately needs to know that he has his parents' unconditional love and acceptance. Bullying can happen to anyone, at any time, and the victim needs all the support he can get if he is to emerge from the experience with his self-esteem and confidence intact.

All these conflicting feelings and worries, combined with the fact that the child's behaviour at home is probably becoming disruptive and upsetting to everyone else in the family, can prove overwhelming for parents. Probably the best way to cope with this is to find someone who is not involved in the situation, to whom you can unload your feelings of anxiety, confusion and guilt. A good and supportive friend can fulfil this role, but sometimes it is easier to talk to a stranger, and there are several organizations which provide support, advice and counselling for parents in distress listed on pages 109–11. For parents faced with the reality of bullying, though, the most important thing is to remember that you are not powerless to help your child, whether she wants you to get involved or not. There is a great deal you can do to change the situation, as we will see in later chapters, but the first and most important steps to helping your child are:

- Know the signs that indicate bullying.
- Understand that your child may find it difficult to talk about what is worrying her, and be prepared to help her or to find out in other ways.
- If and when she does talk, listen to your child and take the problem seriously.

- Let your child know right away that you will do whatever is necessary to stop the bullying.
- Be aware that you may need help in coping with your own reactions, and try not to let them get in the way of your child's best interests – you're all she's got!

4

What parents can do

So, you have established that your child is being bullied. The first step towards helping him is to take the problem seriously. Reassure him that you will do all that you can to make sure that he isn't bullied again, and then take the time to get the facts as straight as possible. Don't agree to keep school bullying a secret: explain carefully to your child that the bully will certainly go on to bully other children too, if he is allowed to get away with it, and that the only way to stop the problem once and for all is to bring it out into the open. Tell him that you and his teachers will make certain that he suffers no reprisals.

As we have seen, the discovery that your child is being bullied can leave you paralysed with shock and anger – but you are not powerless to help. We will look at how best parents can approach the school for help, and what action you can expect them to take, in the following chapters. In this chapter, we will discuss strategies that your child can use to deal with bullies, and ways in which you can help her to develop the confidence she needs to avoid a recurrence of the problem in the future. You may have other children who have not been bullied, or who are too young to have started school. Why wait until trouble arises? Most children will have a brush with the bully at some time during school life, and a bit of preparation can make the difference between a frightening and humiliating experience, and another of life's obstacles successfully negotiated, with all the benefits to self-confidencce that entails. Getting the whole family involved in the role-plays, activities and discussions below can provide that preparation.

First, let's look at immediate, practical measures for avoiding and discouraging the bully.

Should you teach your child to hit back?

Hitting back at the bully can sometimes work, but it could also get your child into worse trouble. A small child being picked on by a larger one, or a single child being picked on by a group, is likely to come off worst if the situation escalates into a free-for-all. Most bullies target children who are smaller and weaker than themselves, and the odds will usually be stacked against the victim in a fight.

Hitting back can also get the victim into trouble.

> Chris, a single man in his late twenties, told me about the advice he gave to the thirteen-year-old daughter of a friend, who was miserable after suffering persistent bullying at the hands of another girl at school. Her parents were committed Christians, and had advised her to 'turn the other cheek', but the bullying was getting worse and worse and she was getting more and more depressed about it.
>
> I told her, next time it happens, you just hit her as hard as you can and shout 'leave me alone'. The next time I saw the family, two days later, her mother was in a terrible state. She had been summoned to the school in the middle of the day to take her daughter home, because she had given another girl a bloody nose in a playground fight. I felt dreadful; she'd taken my advice and hit back, but she got suspended as a result, and her parents were overwhelmed with shame at what she'd done. The bullying stopped, though, so perhaps it wasn't entirely the wrong thing to do.

Perhaps not, but hitting back is probably best kept as absolutely the last resort. There are many ways, short of physical violence, in which a child can be assertive. Bullies prefer easy targets, and showing that you won't be intimidated easily is often enough to deter them, or at least to avert a confrontation. You can help your child to be more assertive by practising the following strategies with him at home, perhaps acting out the sort of situations he might encounter.

Strategies to beat the bully

Don't look like a victim

Teach your child to appear confident, even if she doesn't feel it – walking with long strides, head erect, shoulders back and looking ahead. She is far less likely to attract the attention of the bullies, who are looking for an easy victim, if she looks confident and purposeful. Practising in front of a mirror will help her to get the confident look right.

Coping with taunts

The best way to deal with name-calling and taunts is to laugh them off or ignore them. This is not the reaction that the bullies expect, and may be enough to discourage them. Telling the children who are bothering him to 'get lost' (choosing his own words, and looking and sounding angry!) and then walking away immediately can also work.

If your child has some physical peculiarity that makes her look different – prominent teeth or a birthmark, for instance – or if she is in a racial minority or has special needs which pick her out from other children, it makes sense to prepare her for the attention that this will inevitably attract.

- Make a list between you of all the taunts he might encounter.
- Have fun together making up some appropriate responses.
- Practise putting these responses into action, with you or a brother or sister play-acting the bully.

The idea is not to get drawn into a slanging-match, but to come up quickly with a well-chosen riposte, and leave before the bully has time to catch her breath. The whole exercise should be fun, and increase the child's confidence in her own ability to cope, and should be abandoned straight away if it becomes a chore or an exercise in which she feels pressured to come up with the 'right' response or risk failure.

You can extend the role-play approach, inventing new situations and experimenting with different strategies. Understanding how the bully sees the situation will help your child, so let him play the bully too! Encourage him to think about how it feels. If he saw two children – one walking purposefully across the playground towards a group of friends and one standing alone and looking nervous – which would he pick on? How would he expect them to react? How would it feel if they reacted differently?

Coping with threats

Name-calling across the playground can be ignored, but being cornered, grabbed or threatened by one or more bullies is altogether more frightening, and calls for a quick and positive response. If threatened in this way, your child should:

- Walk away if possible, looking straight ahead and heading for a group of friends, a teacher or someone else who can help.
- If they try to stop her, shout NO! GO AWAY! then walk away quickly.
- If threatened by a gang, Kidscape suggests looking the weakest one straight in the eye, saying 'this isn't funny', and walking away.

Threats should be reported immediately to a teacher or other adult, and to parents.

Coping with violence

Being shoved, hit and kicked is even more difficult for the victim to deal with. If it is an isolated incident – one blow, perhaps accompanied by some verbal abuse or threats – then it is probably best to react as for threats, and report the incident immediately to an adult. Reacting with violence might make matters worse.

The child who is cornered by a gang of bullies and beaten up, with no help nearby, has a difficult decision to make. He can:

- Protect vulnerable areas of the body as best he can and take the blows in the hope that the bullies will lose interest or someone will come along to stop them.
- Make as much noise as possible in the hope of getting help.
- Fight back and escape as soon as possible.
- Wait for the chance to make a break for it.

Which option, or combination of options, the child takes will depend on her assessment of the situation. Wherever the incident takes place, it is always a good idea to try to attract attention: shouting 'fire' is often more effective than 'help', as people's fears for their property will bring them along to see what's going on far more quickly than the possibility of someone being hurt. The prospect of being caught in the act may discourage the bullies, even if no help appears immediately.

Where there are adults close at hand, in the school playground for instance, it shouldn't be long before someone realizes what's going on and a teacher or supervisor comes along, so it may be worth the child hanging on for a few moments, protecting himself as best he can, rather than escalating the violence by hitting out. A fight will attract a crowd, and the victim can appeal to them to help or to tell someone what's going on.

If there is no help at hand and it looks as though the child is going to get hurt anyway, fighting back may be the only remaining option. Research has shown that attack victims suffer less psychological harm if they have made an attempt to defend themselves, even if it wasn't particularly successful, and there is always the chance that putting up an unexpected fight will discourage the bullies, who really only want an easy time of it, after all. As any self-defence teacher will tell her class, if you are going to hit back at an attacker, it has to hurt enough to stop him in his tracks, at least for long enough for you to get away; hitting him somewhere it only hurts enough to annoy him will just get you a few more kicks and punches, delivered with added determination. If you would like your child to find out more about physical self-defence, find a good self-defence class (see chapter 10) where she will learn to target an attacker's weakest points, as well as a good deal about avoiding trouble in the first place.

There have been a few instances in which school bullies have used weapons to threaten their victims, and there is always the possibility that a bully will pick up a 'weapon of convenience' – perhaps a stone or a bicycle pump – and use it to threaten or attack. Where weapons are involved the threatened child will need to weigh up the situation very carefully before reacting. If she feels that she must fight back or be seriously hurt and there is more than one attacker, the best advice is to go for the one with the weapon first – she can't afford to turn her back on him while she tackles someone else. Again, anyone who is going to take on an armed attacker needs to know what she's doing, and a good self-defence class will teach how to keep an attacker out of range, fight back effectively, break grips, and so on. Sometimes a simple response like spitting in the attacker's face is enough to make him let go or hesitate for a moment – long enough for a quick get away – and won't get the spitter into any trouble herself.

Taking precautions

It is always far easier to stay out of trouble than to tackle it once it has started. If he knows that there are bullies about, your child can take precautions against being singled out for their attention by:

- In the playground, staying with a friend or group of friends. Bullies usually pick on people who are on their own.
- Avoiding predictability. If he walks or cycles to and from school, he could vary his route home and, again, stay with a group if possible.
- Getting used to weighing up potentially dangerous situations, avoiding them if possible, and making a plan of action for use if the worst comes to the worst and he needs to act quickly. Simple measures like making sure that he doesn't let a potential bully get between him and his escape route, or having a good put-down ready to use in response to verbal taunts, will help avoid trouble and give confidence.
- Making sure that he reports any bullying he witnesses, even if he or his friends are not involved at all. If the bully is allowed to continue, your child could be his next victim.

Should parents tackle the bullies themselves?

Some parents have done just this very successfully: buttonholed the bullies and told them, in no uncertain terms, that they will be answerable to their victim's mum, dad or big brothers and sisters if they ever go near her again.

Talking, or threatening to talk to, the 'bullies' parents can also work very effectively although it does need to be handled with some discretion. Most parents will need a bit of space to get over their shock at the suggestion that their child could have done something wrong before they can begin to think rationally about the situation. They may never reach this point if your initial approach forces them into an aggressive stance from which they cannot back down without loss of face. Approaching the parents of the bully (or perhaps, at this stage, we should say the alleged bully) with a suggestion that, 'There seems to be a bit of trouble between our kids, let's talk it over and arrive at some solution' can, however, yield very useful results. There are drawbacks to the purely 'do-it-yourself' approach, though: if the bullying is taking place in school, the school needs to know about it and to take an active part in putting a stop to the bully's activities, or the bully will simply turn his attentions to another child with less assertive parents. For the bullied child, the prospect of having a parent wade in and sort out his battles for him can be acutely and unbearably embarrassing, although he may come to terms with this in the end if the bullying stops as a result.

If you do decide to tackle the bullies on your child's behalf, do bear in mind the possibility that you will lay yourself open to charges of assault if you manhandle them in any way, or even threaten harm without actually laying a finger on them. There is always the possibility, too, that you will escalate a case of bullying into a family feud. On balance, it is probably better to let the school, or even the police, handle things for you if possible.

Longer-term measures: what if it's her fault?

Some bullying is entirely random, but in a few cases the bullied child has some supremely annoying or offensive habit which provokes other children to bully her. We all remember that boy at school who picked his ears constantly, the girl who didn't use deodorant. Then there was the one who butted into everybody's conversations, and always had to have the last word. We find these things irritating in others as adults, so why should children find them any less annoying? Not all irritating little habits are as obvious as these examples, and when it comes to our own children, we often actually find endearing the little quirks that other children might look on as odd. Look objectively at your child (yes, I know that's a tall order), and ask yourself whether there is anything about her behaviour and social accomplishments that other children might frown upon. Does she suck her thumb or pick her nose – does she find sharing difficult, or get upset and aggressive if she loses a game or an argument? If you can identify an area that might be causing problems, you can point this out to her gently – certainly more gently than her peers might – and help her to modify her behaviour, at least when she is with her friends and classmates. Even younger children are capable of understanding that some behaviour is inappropriate in some situations, and will be glad to find a way of fitting in better with their peers.

Building confidence

More often, where a child is bullied persistently, it is simply a lack of self-confidence that makes him attractive as a target. Following the guidelines for family life outlined in chapter 5 will give your child a head start in this respect, but it doesn't take much to dent a child's self-confidence, and many of the influences on your child's life are outside your control. Building self-esteem is a long, slow job, particularly where it has been broken down by rejection and intimidation by other children, but you can help your child back on the road to confidence again.

First, and most important, every child needs the unconditional acceptance and love of her parents. When the rest of the world seems to despise you (and a child's peer group is the rest of the world as far as the child is concerned), it helps a lot to know that there is someone you can absolutely rely on for support and love, however worthless you feel.

If your child needs her confidence boosted:

- Tell her again and again 'I think you are a really great person' – you can't do this too often. Your child may not look thrilled, but will feel enormously relieved.
- Find and encourage your child's strengths, and give her due credit for them, and for trying even when she doesn't succeed. Lack of confidence makes it enormously difficult to take the risk of failure, and your child may need a very great deal of encouragement and support to try anything new.
- Don't try to 'toughen her up' by thrusting her into overly challenging situations. Time enough for these when she is feeling more confident.
- Acknowledge your child's fears. Don't brush them aside with admonishments to 'stop being silly' or 'pull yourself together'. Remember, she doesn't want to feel anxious or afraid any more than you want her to.
- Don't despair. She will gain confidence eventually with the right support, and all the quicker if allowed to do so in her own time.

Activities

Taking part in activities outside home and school can help to build confidence, and give the opportunity to make fresh relationships with other children, often in a better-supervised environment than most schools can provide. Though by no means an exhaustive list, the following might give you some ideas for activities that might help your child to build confidence and make friends.

Drama and role-play

Drama clubs can give children the chance to explore roles, situations and relationships in a controlled and structured environment, but you need to choose your group carefully. Some groups, often those taking place within a stage school, focus almost entirely on putting on productions, and are looking for members who want to be on stage. This approach is fine for some children, but opens the way to failure for the less confident child, who may not be 'star' material. Other groups, although they will put on productions from time to time, concentrate on developing the potential of each child through games, drama and role-play. Such groups are often held within local authority youth centres and are affiliated to the National Association of Youth Theatres. Your local authority Drama Advisor or the drama teacher at your child's school should be able to put you in touch with a suitable group, or you may find details in your local library or Youth and Community Centre. The NAYT (address on page 111) will supply you with details of affiliated groups in your area.

The best way to tell which sort of group you have found is to talk to the leader for a few minutes. If he starts talking about mammoth productions, agencies and the number of children who have gone on to get acting jobs, the chances are that this is not the group for your child. If, on the other hand, the leader talks about personal development and chooses productions in which all children can be involved, regardless of their talent or lack of it, you could be on to a winner. Tell the leader about your concerns for your child. A good group leader will be able to introduce activities that will help build his confidence, and will keep an eye out for problems within the group that might affect your child.

Sports

Research by the National Coaching Foundation has shown that young people who take part in sports have a stronger psychological profile than others. In simple terms, this means that they will be able to respond more positively to the challenges life faces them with. Not every child will be interested in taking up a sport, but a bit of encouragement might get your child started on a hobby that will provide her with new friends, a manageable challenge and a sense of achievement which will carry on into adult years.

Some clubs welcome the recreational player, whilst others are concerned solely with competitive success. The latter sort of club can be great for the talented and ambitious child, but the less confident child, who simply wants to have fun and build confidence, may feel left out or rejected in an atmosphere where winning is everything. This won't help self-confidence. A tough sport won't necessarily produce a tough child! Sending an anxious and physically timid child to a rugby club could annihilate what confidence he has; a non-contact sport like table-tennis or swimming might be more appropriate.

Always choose a club in which the instructors are qualified to coach within the appropriate governing body for their sport. For a list of sports clubs in your area, contact the Sports Council (address on page 111). For guidance on choosing a martial arts or self-defence club, see chapter 10.

Youth clubs

Youth clubs today are very different from those of twenty years ago. Rather than simply getting a group of kids together for a game of ping-pong, a drink of squash and the occasional disco, today's youth worker is trained to provide activities that encourage the full social and personal development of the individual, including group discussions and activities focusing on bullying, sexism and a host of other important issues. A well-run group can provide the opportunity for mixing with new people in a controlled environment, and the opportunity to try new activities within the security of the group.

Youth groups

Most areas boast a variety of voluntary youth groups:

Cubs
Scouts
Brownies
Guides
Boys' and Girls' Brigades
Red Cross and St John Ambulance
Church groups and Sunday Schools
Sea and Air Scouts, Sea Cadets, Combined Cadet Force, etc.

There are many more, and you will find details of groups in your area in the local paper or library. Many of these groups run a graduated system of awards or badges, providing the opportunity for every child, whatever their talents, to gain a feeling of achievement and progress and so build confidence. The people who run them are usually dedicated and experienced, and small groups can provide an almost family-like environment in which even the most timid child can flourish and develop. It is always worth discussing any anxieties you may have about your child with the group leader, who may be able to offer insights into her interaction with the group, and can keep an eye out for problems.

Someone to talk to

Children who are or have been involved in bullying can be weighed down with worries and concerns: Why did it happen to me – is there something wrong with me? Is it all right to be a sneak, and will anyone ever talk to me again if I do tell? I know it was wrong to join in with the bullying. Does that mean that I'm a bad person? Sharing the burden of worries with someone else can help your child to sort out how he really feels, change what can be changed about the situation and come to terms with what can't. The trouble is that it isn't always easy to talk to family, or even friends, about something that's really important to you, especially if it involves doubts about yourself. If your child needs to talk to you, or if you feel the need of some emotional support yourself, you could try the following sources of help.

● *Child Guidance Service*

Your family doctor can refer your child to a Child Guidance Clinic for help, or you can contact them yourself if you prefer. The Child Guidance Service helps with family problems of all sorts, and is free. You will find details of your local clinic listed under the name of your local authority in the telephone book.

● *Youth counselling*

Most large towns will have a Youth Counselling centre. Known simply by their house number, e.g., 'No. 22', these centres open at times when children and young people are able to attend, and provide free, trained and experienced counselling for all sorts of problems. Youth counsellors are also available in some schools, although children might prefer that their friends didn't know they were seeing a counsellor. You can make the first contact with the counselling centre, and take your child to counselling sessions, but what passes between counsellor and client is confidential, so don't expect to be kept informed.

- *The Samaritans*

The Samaritans provide free, confidential help for anyone who is under stress, and are most suitable for parents and older children. First contact is usually by telephone, but it is possible to meet a Samaritan face to face to talk about your worries. Most towns will have a branch of The Samaritans, which you will find listed in your telephone directory.

- *Childline*

Childline provides counselling help over the telephone for children up to eighteen years old who are suffering abuse, bullying or other problems.

- *Youth Access*

This is a counselling agency for young people which will be able to put you in touch with a counsellor in your area. Some counsellors, such as those based in the Youth Counselling centres mentioned above, will provide their services free, some will make a negotiable charge, according to means, and some will be quite expensive. It is best to ask any counsellor you contact from the outset what her charges will be.

Parents know best

As we've seen, there is a great deal you can do to help your child cope with bullying – in fact, you are your child's lifeline, and the only people who know and care deeply enough to judge just what his needs are in the present situation. Don't be discouraged from doing what you feel is right for him by teachers, friends, relatives or anyone else who might try to influence your decisions. By all means listen to and consider what they have to say and examine all the possible options carefully, but remember that no one knows your child as you do, however much they know about children in general.

- Give your child unconditional support and understanding.
- Keep him off school if you think the situation warrants it.
- Reassure him that you will protect him from further bullying.
- Help him to develop strategies to avoid or discourage the bully.
- Help him to build or rebuild his confidence and make new friends.
- Give him the opportunity to find support outside the family if he finds this easier.

5

A good start

You can be sure that your child will experience bullying at some time during her childhood, whether as victim, bully or bystander. While there is nothing you can do to prevent this, there is a great deal you can do to lessen the likelihood of her becoming a bully herself, and to give her the confidence and resilience she needs to cope with teasing and bullying from other children.

Bullying is an aggressive act. We can't keep aggression out of our children's lives altogether, nor would it be a good idea to do so if we could; aggression can be channelled usefully to provide the driving force that helps people achieve their goals in life. We can, however, help our children learn to understand and control their aggressive impulses, and avoid putting them into situations where an aggressive response is inevitable.

What is aggression?

Psychology textbooks define aggression as 'a response that delivers noxious stimuli to another organism'. In plain English, 'noxious stimuli' means anything that causes physical or psychological harm: a blow, a taunt, or even something much less direct like spreading rumours or writing nasty letters. Aggression is not as simple a response as it might appear, and aggressive acts are often inspired by a mixture of many emotions: anger, jealousy, fear, hate, frustration and many others can all play a part.

We all experience these emotions from time to time, so what makes one child react aggressively to even minor upsets while others seem to take life's ups and downs in her stride? A tendency towards aggressive behaviour can be caused by a number of factors:

- *Heredity*. Some children are born with more potential for aggression than others, even within the same family.

- *Sex*. Boys are generally more aggressive than girls.

- *Upbringing*. Children brought up in a family where aggression is the norm will themselves adopt aggressive behaviour.

52

- *Environment.* Stress, unhappiness, anxiety, frustration and fear can all trigger off aggressive behaviour.

- *Example.* Research has shown that exposure to violence on TV films and even cartoons can encourage aggression.

Aggressive behaviour itself has two main forms.

Affective aggression.
This is the sort of aggressive behaviour that is triggered off by strong feelings of anger and provocation. E.g., one child hits another because she has taken her sweets.

Instrumental aggression.
This is aggressive behaviour used as a means to an end, without direct feelings of provocation or anger against the victim. e.g., one child threatens another in order to make him hand over his skateboard.

If all aggressive behaviour were as straightforward as the above examples suggest, it would be relatively easy for parents and teachers to handle. The problem is that much of what seems to be instrumental aggression – threats, abuse and violence against people that the bully has no direct quarrel with – is in fact the result of suppressed anger and frustration about something else in her life that she feels powerless to change. The child who is being bullied by a big brother, for example, may 'take it out' later on another child, or the three-year-old with a new baby sister may show no signs of resenting the new baby, but become a terror at playgroup.

Whether your child is naturally placid and slow to anger, or quick-tempered and volatile, the way you bring him up will help him learn to understand and cope with his own aggressive feelings and those of others.

Handling aggression in young children: dealing with tantrums

Feelings of jealousy, anger and aggression can be overwhelmingly powerful and very frightening, and nothing illustrates this as clearly as the two-year-old throwing a tantrum. She is so gripped with fury that she completely loses control of herself. For a while, she wants to destroy everything around her – including her mother, the most important person in her life and the symbol of all her security. For all she knows, she may be capable of such destruction, and immediately after the tantrum passes she feels devastated and afraid at what she might have done. Soon however, she finds that however destructive she felt, the world is still there, and her mother still loves her. This knowledge and the confidence it brings lessens the power her emotions have over her, and she begins to learn control.

Difficult though it is to cope with a screaming toddler in the bus queue, tantrums need to be handled with great restraint. If you react violently to his rage, shout, smack or, even worse, reject him afterwards, you will confirm his own worst fears that his feelings of anger are dangerous, making it far harder for him to gain control over them. He needs to be restrained, for his own safety and to avoid too much inconvenience to others, but it is important that his carer remains calm and unaffected by his rage. When he has calmed down, he will need reassurance that everything is all right – a cuddle says this perfectly.

You are likely to be the first human target of your child's aggression, usually at around the age of two years. Life is full of frustrations for a two-year-old: she wants lots of things – a biscuit, freedom from your restraining hand, to climb on to that windowsill and look out of the open window – and she wants them *now*. Often, you are the only thing standing between her and what she wants, and hitting you is an immediate way to get your attention and, she hopes, get what she wants. If it works, hitting will soon become an established part of her repertoire, and she will extend its use to others in and outside the family. If you are to avoid this, you need to show her from the start that hitting is definitely 'out of order'.

- DO pull away from her quickly.
- DO exclaim 'No' loudly and in a shocked tone.
- DON'T laugh at her comical attempts at coercion.
- DON'T hit back.

If you smack your child as a way of getting her to listen to you or do what you want, you can hardly blame her if she tries the same tactics on you and, eventually, on others.

Problems in the early years

Problems with aggression may arise during your child's pre-school years. True bullying is rare in playgroups and nurseries. When under-fives are aggressive, it is generally in response to an immediate overwhelming desire to get or keep something – shoving away the child who wants a turn with the best dumper-truck, for instance – or shows itself as a general tendency to carry boisterous games too far. Few pre-school children are capable of the circumspection necessary to conceal their behaviour from adults, nor do they wish to, so this sort of behaviour is usually easy for staff to detect, and it is rare for any one child to be picked on exclusively. An unduly aggressive child at playgroup, however, can be a real nightmare for staff and children alike, and needs help to control his aggression at home and in the group if he is not to have problems throughout his school life.

First, it is important to try and identify the cause of the problem. Where a pre-school child is unusually aggressive, it is often because of some temporary stress: illness, moving house or a new baby. Jane, a playgroup helper, describes the behaviour of a three-and-a-half-year-old girl at her playgroup.

Clare looked like a little angel – tiny, with a sweet, round face, big blue eyes and curly blonde hair – and it took us a while to realize what was going on. At first she was fine, but then her mother got pregnant again. Perhaps she felt tired and wasn't able to give Clare so much time, or perhaps they just told her about it too soon, and the thought of a new baby taking some of her parents' attention away from her was too much for her, but she changed almost overnight. She really seemed to want to hurt the other children. I caught her with one little girl's head trapped in the wendy house door. She knew that it was hurting her – the child was screaming – but she was pulling it shut on her head as hard as she could. She would deliberately tread on other children's fingers when they were playing on the floor, run the dolls' pushchairs into their legs, and pinch whoever she was sitting next to round the tables. We had to watch her all the time. The supervisor talked to her mother, but she said she hadn't noticed anything wrong, and didn't think that she was particu-larly worried about anything at home. It got so bad that even the other mothers started talking about her, and in the end she just didn't come back to the playgroup. I heard that her mother had got her into a local nursery – perhaps she was embarrassed by Clare's behaviour, although I didn't think that she ever really believed she was as bad as we said she was.

Clare must have felt very angry indeed with her mother, but she also loved her and couldn't express her angry feelings to her directly – instead, she transferred her anger to other children at playgroup. She needed help to express her fears and anger in other ways, perhaps through play as outlined in chapter 3, and lots of reassurance from her parents that they still loved and valued her.

Sometimes a pre-school child's aggression is a reaction to the treatment she is experiencing from someone else, another adult or child in or outside the family. If your child's behaviour changes suddenly and inexplicably, it is always worth considering the possibility that someone – a brother or sister, childminder or even a grandparent –is bullying or abusing her in some way.

If your pre-school child is going through an aggressive phase, there are several things you can do to get the situation under control while you try to sort out the underlying problem:

- Put playgroup or nursery staff, childminder or other caretakers in the picture, and establish a consistent policy for dealing with aggressive behaviour.
- Make sure that your child is supervised in all situations where she may become aggressive.
- If trouble flares, remove your child quickly and calmly from the scene of the conflict and make it clear that she can't return until she is prepared to behave sensibly.

Responding to aggressive behaviour with aggression of your own – shouting, smacking, shaking or 'giving them a taste of their own medicine' by literally biting back (yes, some parents have tried this!) will simply make matters worse.

Family teasing and arguments

Even if it were possible to prevent our children from teasing and arguing with one another, we would be unwise to do so. The family provides training for life in an environment where most of our experiments and mistakes will be tolerated, and in it we learn to cope with the stresses, strains and conflicts that inevitably arise between people who live, work or play together. We also learn from our families to understand and, to some extent, control the very strong emotions that these relationships arouse in us. If we try to stamp out every trace of conflict, ban arguments and fights, and outlaw teasing, we will produce children who are singularly ill-equipped to survive amongst others who are accustomed to using these things in daily life.

Problems can arise, however, when teasing and arguing are allowed to go too far, and it is important that everyone in the family understands when 'enough is enough'. As a rule-of-thumb, teasing has gone too far when:

- someone gets really upset;
- someone gets really angry;
- the same person is always on the receiving end;
- the teasing concerns something about which the 'teasee' is already worried or anxious.

An argument has gone too far when:

- someone gets really upset or frightened;
- someone loses their temper and starts hitting, pushing or throwing things;
- the arguers forget what they were arguing about and start hurling damaging personal insults.

When teasing or arguments get out of hand, it is time for parents to step in. If tempers have been lost in an argument, it is probably best to separate the children concerned, and deal with the subject of the argument yourself – the 'If you can't share, then neither of you are going to have it' approach – or to postpone settlement until they have both calmed down enough to discuss it sensibly. Where teasing has gone too far, the teaser will usually know that they have overstepped the family's bounds of behaviour, but may need reminding that they were causing real distress.

Talking about worries

There are very good reasons for encouraging your child to talk to you about his feelings right from the earliest years:

- It takes practise to find the words to describe how you are feeling.
- Talking about your feelings helps you to understand and cope with them.

- Knowing that someone else is aware of your worries and wants to help makes you feel better.
- Children sometimes need reassurance that the way they feel is normal.

Things that feel really important can be very hard to talk about, but you can only help your child with her problems effectively if you know what is going on, particularly where bullying is concerned. If talking about things is the established way of coping in your family, there is a much better chance that your child will turn to you in a crisis. You can encourage this from the start:

- Make some time every day to talk with your child about what she has done and felt. Bathtime is a good opportunity to talk to the younger child: 'What did we do today? We went to the shops, didn't we? And what did we buy?' For the school-age child, teatime or bedtime could be your time for going over the day's activities.

- Listen. It is all too easy to let your mind wander to what's for supper or whether there are enough shirts ironed for tomorrow, and miss something significant or important in your child's blow-by-blow account of the day's activities.

- Tell your child how you feel, and share some (but obviously not all) of your own concerns. She will learn from you the language and concepts she needs to describe her own feelings.

Accepting feelings

Part of listening to your child is accepting the way he says he feels. If you don't, he will not only feel frustrated and angry, but will eventually give up trying to tell you how he feels altogether. This may sound obvious, but how often have you heard the following exchanges:

FOUR-YEAR-OLD: Mum, it's boring here. I want to go home.
MUM: No you don't.

EIGHT-YEAR-OLD: I hate my big brother, I wish he'd go and live somewhere else.
DAD: Don't say things like that. You know you don't mean it.

TWELVE-YEAR-OLD: Mum, I don't want to go to that school any more – I don't like it.
MUM: Nonsense, you've always loved it there!

It is much more helpful to the child if you can accept the way he feels at the moment, sympathize, and help him to explore his feelings further, and perhaps find a solution to the underlying problem. Some more helpful responses might be:

- 'There isn't much here for you to do, is there? We will be going home for tea when I've finished talking to Grandma, but perhaps we can find you something to do until then.'

- 'It must make you feel very angry when he won't let you join in his games. Come and help me in the garden for a while – I'm sure that he will play with you again later, when he has finished what he's doing.'

- 'You look upset. Tell me what's happened to make you feel like this.'

Be positive

Telling children where they have gone wrong is not enough. If we want to get the best out of our children, we must at the very least balance our criticism for what they get wrong with praise for what they get right. This can sometimes be extraordinarily difficult, particularly for parents who are tired, angry, or preoccupied with problems of their own.

It only takes a little ingenuity and self-control to turn a potentially negative situation into one which leaves your child feeling good about herself *and* doing what you want. What's more, you can cut out a good deal of the strain of parenting by averting conflict before it starts, rather than dealing with it after it has arisen. Supposing, for instance, your three-year-old is playing on the swings in the park, and it is time to go home.

MUM: Come on, it's time to go home.
CHILD: No, don't want to go.
MUM: Well we've got to go. I've got to get something for Daddy's tea. Come on.
CHILD: Not yet.

MUM: Yes, now! Don't be naughty.
CHILD: (struggling to get away): NO! Don't want to . . .
MUM: Behave yourself. I'm going to get very cross with you in a minute. COME ON.

And so it goes on, all the way home. You know that your child will not want to leave, so why not take a more positive approach:

MUM: We've got to get something for Daddy's tea. I don't know what to get. Could you help me choose?
CHILD: Yes. Daddy likes fish.
MUM: Yes, so he does – you clever girl. Let's go to the shop and see if they've got any. If they haven't, perhaps you could help me choose something else.

All right, it isn't always as easy as that, but it will cut out much of the strain on yourself and your child if you make it easy, and rewarding in terms of approval and self-respect, for her to do the right thing. There is nothing to be gained from direct confrontation, which will usually result in your using superior physical strength to get what you want – not an example that most of us would wish to set our children. Of course, it is important that the end result is your child doing what you asked her to do in the first place, and if your efforts to make this easy for her fail, you may have to resort to saying, 'I know that you don't want to do what I have asked, but sometimes we all have to do things we don't want. Please do it NOW.' With luck, though, you won't have to do this very often, and your child will take you very seriously when you do.

Something to build on

Children can be infuriating at times, and how we react to their mistakes can be very important to their self-image. Four-year-old Sally has knocked over a pot plant whilst trying to sweep the floor with a full-size broom.

1. MUM: Oh no. You stupid girl. Why can't you be more careful! You're always doing things like this. Just look at the mess you've made – and you're not the one who has to clear it up. I've got all this work to do, and now I'll have to do this as well. I'm really cross with you – go to your room.

2. MUM: Oh no – my favourite plant. That broom is really much too big for you. You can't tell what the other end is doing because it sticks out so far. If you want to help with the sweeping, it would be better if you used the dustpan and brush. Let's get it and sweep up this mess now.

In the first instance, Sally is left feeling bad about herself. She has learned that she is stupid and clumsy, and her mother has given her no way out of the predicament.

In the second, Sally's mother has shown that she is upset about the plant – Sally would be surprised and anxious if she didn't – but she understands that it was an accident, and has both given Sally the information she needs to avoid it happening again, by using the dustpan and brush instead of the big broom, and the chance to help put right the damage she has done.

Although they both regret the accident, Sally emerges with her self-respect and confidence intact, and having learned a useful lesson for the future. Of course, it would be unrealistic to expect that Sally would never make the same mistake again – often it takes many such experiences to change a child's behaviour permanently – but used consistently this approach will help a child to use her own judgement to weigh up both familiar and unfamiliar situations, and to gain the confidence that she can get things right with a bit of effort.

Expect the best

In some families, children are never given the benefit of the doubt. Often, adults need someone to blame when something goes wrong; after all, if they didn't blame someone else quickly, they might have to admit to being at fault themselves. Children make easy scapegoats, and sometimes the whole family will tacitly elect just one of their number to take the blame for more or less everything that goes wrong.

A typical exchange in such a family goes something like this:

DAD: Where's my spanner?
MUM: I don't know. Have you looked in the garage?
DAD: It's not there. It's gone. I'll bet that James has had it again.
MUM: You could have left it in the greenhouse when you fixed the heater.

DAD: Of course I didn't! No, it'll be James again – he never puts anything back where he found it. James! Where have you put my spanner?

Faced with such low expectations, James will probably live down to them – his dad will think the worst of him whatever he does, so why bother to try? Getting the best out of your child means giving him every opportunity to do the right thing, respecting him enough to believe that he can and will do it most of the time and telling him how pleased and proud you are when he does. If you can do this, he will live up to your expectations – most of the time.

In any transaction with your child, the aim should be to leave him feeling good about himself, even if he feels bad about something he has done, and believing in his own potential to do better next time. Low self-esteem makes both bullies and victims, and building your child's confidence and self-respect will go a long way towards protecting him from aggression – both his own and others'.

Be consistent

Children need the security that a consistent set of family rules and values brings. Difficult though it sometimes is, once we have made a rule or demand it is important that we enforce it consistently and see it through to completion, even when this means more work or time wasted for us. If you have told your child to pick up her toys from the living room floor, for instance, it is important that she does so, even if this means half an hour falling over them while she complains and dithers about where they should go. All right, so you could have done it yourself in five minutes, but then what would she have learned? That if she ignores your instructions for long enough, or complains hard enough about them, she will get away with not doing as she was asked. Next time, you will have to ask more often, shout louder, or threaten with more extreme punishment if she doesn't do as you ask.

However much your child complains about what you ask him to do, self-respect is built on fulfilling our obligations and responsibilities in life. The child who is allowed to let things slide will inevitably feel anxious about his worth as a person, and may fail to appreciate that his actions are important, and that what he does or fails to do has consequences, both for himself and others. As we have seen, a sense of self-worth and responsibility are vital elements in a child's defences against bullying.

It's OK to be human

Perfect parenting is impossible, and parents can only do the best they can within their own limitations. We all find that we are more easily irritated at some times than others; tiredness, PMT and job or money worries can lower any parent's annoyance threshold considerably. If you know that you are under stress, and will not be able to avoid snapping at your child if she whines or misbehaves, it will make life a lot easier for her if you tell her so. Simply saying, 'Look, I'm feeling in a really bad mood/I've got a splitting headache, and it'd be best if you didn't annoy me right now', is enough to give your child fair warning. Even if she persists, and you lose your temper, she will at least know that it isn't all her fault. It's OK for parents to make mistakes as long as they don't pretend to be perfect, and apologizing to your child when you do sets the best example she could possibly have for handling her own mistakes.

Actions have consequences

Left unchecked, it is easy for children to fall into the habit of being nasty to each other without thinking. For instance, six-year-old Matt shows his big brother the model he made at school; big brother comments: 'It's pathetic just like you, stupid'. He probably doesn't really mean to hurt, but his opinion is important to Matt, whose self-esteem and confidence suffer a body-blow.

Everyone needs to learn that their actions, even though they might seem trivial at the time, have consequences for themselves and others, and parents can help by making sure that their children face up to this. The best way to bring this point home is to see that the child who has teased, pushed, taken possessions or whatever makes amends to the child he has hurt. Depending on the severity of his actions, he could:

- apologize to the aggrieved child face to face;
- make a written apology;
- perform a service for the person he's hurt – clean his bike, make his bed, etc.;
- forfeit a possession or pocket money to the aggrieved child;

● buy a present.

It is important that whatever the child is expected to do clearly carries some benefit for the victim. The point you are trying to establish is that someone has suffered as a result of his actions, and that this entails a responsibility to make things right. Punishment alone – missing a favourite TV programme or having pocket money stopped – doesn't carry the same message.

A note on further reading

Family relationships and child-rearing are huge subjects in themselves. In this chapter I have illustrated some of the more common situations within families that can predispose to problems with aggression and bullying, and suggested ways in which they might be approached more positively. I hope that these examples will inspire parents to learn more, and I have included a reading list at the end of this book for those who want to carry their interest further. I particularly recommend the work of Dr John Pearce who, as well as producing the excellent little book *Fighting, Teasing and Bullying*, has published titles like *Tantrums and Tempers*, *Bad Behaviour*, and *Worries and Fears* – subjects of interest to all parents.

Be prepared

Most children will experience bullying at some time during their childhood. Some will take it in their stride, with only minor upset, while for some it will become a major problem, or a way of life. Children who have learned within the family to handle anger, conflict and aggression, who feel generally good about themselves, and who can turn to their parents for help with problems they can't handle themselves, will be well prepared for whatever life throws at them. As we have seen in this chapter, you can help your child in the following ways:

● Set the right example. Bullying behaviour by parents and siblings encourages bullying by the victim.
● Help her to feel good about herself. Find areas where she can feel successful, support her in those where she is having difficulties, and make her feel an important part of the family.
● Provide her with clear and consistent standards of behaviour,

64

and reinforce her good behaviour with praise as well as stopping unacceptable behaviour immediately.

- Listen to her and respect the feelings she expresses, even if you think they are unreasonable.

6
School and pre-school bullying

True bullying amongst pre-school children is rare, as we saw in chapter 5, but child protection agencies are seeing a steady increase in the number of calls concerning bullying received from parents of under-fives. Kidscape feels that pre-school education could play a vital role in reducing bullying in schools, and would like to see more playgroup and nursery staff taking part in its anti-bullying programmes. Perhaps because bullying is not seen as a problem in most playgroups and nurseries, a golden opportunity for early prevention is often missed.

Pre-school bullying

Playgroup or nursery provides for the development of your child's pre-reading, pre-mathematical and other skills through play, in the form of sorting, matching, shape recognition and many other experiences; but pre-school experiences are not all positive. In a poorly run or ill-supervised group, your child can also develop pre-bullying skills, or learn how it feels to be a victim or a failure. A poor choice of playgroup or nursery could start him off on the wrong road for life, so what should you look for when you 'do the rounds' of your local groups?

● *Supervision*

There are regulations governing the ratio of staff to children in pre-school groups, but these are of little use if three of the four adults present are chatting over a cup of coffee in the kitchen. Aggressive behaviour will flourish where supervision is inadequate.

● *Involvement*

Playgroup and nursery staff are there for the benefit of the children. They should be spread about the room, getting involved with what the children are doing – helping when asked, answering questions, encouraging conversation, providing materials, making sure everyone takes turns and no one gets pushed around or left out. If staff regularly congregate around one table, deep in conversation, they are not giving the children the attention they deserve.

● *Environment*

Surroundings should be kept clean and tidy, and equipment in good condition. Broken toys, puzzles with pieces missing, useless scissors, blunt pencils cause frustration, disappointment and discouragement, and should not be presented for children's use.

● *Discipline*

If staff often have to shout to keep order, to give lectures or tickings-off, or to use punishments like a 'naughty chair', they are probably making some basic mistakes in the running of the group. Older and more boisterous children should be kept under control, because they can distress and frighten younger and less confident members of the group, but the principal means of dealing with excessive noise or rumbustious behaviour should be to channel it into a new and interesting activity; this can be as simple as clearing one table and bringing out a fresh set of toys, or taking everyone outside for some ball games. A good group will have a busy but not frantic atmosphere, with very little overt discipline in evidence. Each group should have a clearly-defined policy for dealing with arguments and fights, and should be able to tell you what that policy is.

● *Valuing individuals*

Unlike schools, playgroups and nurseries do not have educational targets to meet or results to publish, so there is plenty of room for each child to develop at her own pace, and to be valued for who she is, not what she can do. There is no hurry for children to produce presentable 'work', paint recognizable pictures, write their names, colour inside the lines or any of the other things that parents and staff sometimes think are so important.

Pre-school children need encouragement to try new things, and plenty of praise for their achievements, however insignificant they may seem to an adult. What they don't need is pressure to succeed, which carries with it the equal chance of failure and long-term damage to self-esteem. Comments like 'What's this picture supposed to be then?', 'If that's supposed to be a house, where are the windows?' and 'That's not a proper car, it's only got three wheels' are distinctly unhelpful at this stage, as is the playgroup helper who carefully tidies up each child's mother's day card, so that it will be 'good enough' to take home! The pictures on display in the group should be the work of the children, with all the painting-over-the-lines, weird colour schemes, runs, spots, smudges and three-eared bunnies that entails.

Feeling good about yourself is a child's first line of defence against bullying, as we saw in chapter 2, and the pre-school group has an important role to play in building children's confidence, self-esteem and social skills.

Primary-school bullying

Bullying starts in earnest after the move to primary school. In contrast to the pre-school group, 'Big school' brings together more children over a broader age-range with less supervision, and a power struggle begins into which most children are drawn one way or another. The focus of a child's life shifts away from home and family, and being accepted by peers assumes an ever greater importance. Children quickly discover that they feel even more a part of their group if there are others who are emphatically *not* a part of that group, and that having a common 'enemy' makes them feel closer to their friends.

The reception class will swiftly sort itself out into a complex hierarchy and, although there will be shifts in the balance of power from time to time, many children will assume a position in the pecking order that will carry them through their primary school years, and may even follow them between schools and into their secondary-school life – not a pleasant prospect for those at the bottom of the heap.

In these conditions, bullying progresses beyond the odd push and the occasional outburst of temper. School-age children soon learn to 'push each other's crumple buttons'. Worse still, they learn to keep their activities secret from adults, and sustained, physical and non-physical bullying becomes an increasing possibility. The differences between boys and girls start to become apparent, with girls tending towards non-physical, and boys towards physical bullying.

The factors that encourage bullying in schools have been clearly identified, and parents can minimize the chances of their child suffering serious problems with bullying by choosing a school that understands the problem, and tackles it in a positive way (see

'Choosing schools' later in this chapter). Unfortunately, making it through primary school without problems is no guarantee of a trouble-free time after the big move to secondary school.

The transition from primary to secondary school – a danger point

As we have seen, patterns of bullying are often established during the pre- and primary-school years, and some parents will be aware even before their children start secondary school that they are likely to need extra support and practical help if they are to avoid problems in this new environment. The transition from primary to secondary school, with all its attendant upheaval, can mean both a new start for the child who has become locked into the role of victim in primary-school life, and the beginning of a downward slide for the child who has sailed through primary school without problems.

Children who have already experienced bullying as victims in primary school may take the opportunity to become bullies in secondary school, tagging along with groups of stronger children, or being accepted by the children who bullied them before on condition that they join in their behaviour – after all, they've played the game before and know the rules. This is what happened to Tony, as his mother explains:

Tony was pretty unhappy for his last two years at primary school. He was picked on regularly by a group of three boys in his class – not physically, but they used to call him things like 'wobble bottom', because he was a bit overweight, and they wouldn't let him join in their games in the playground. I was worried when he told me that these boys would be going to the same secondary school as him, and even thought about sending him to a different school, but that would have meant a long journey each morning and afternoon to get him there and back, and he didn't really want to go to a school where he wouldn't know anybody anyway, so he ended up in the first year with these same three boys.

It really surprised me in his first term when he kept mentioning their names – it was obvious that he was spending quite a bit of time with them. I was really relieved – he seemed happier at last, and it looked as though we had made the right decision. Then I got a call from the school – his class tutor wanted to see me. She told me that he and these other boys had been picking on another first year, apparently a quiet boy from a different primary school. Once I got over my surprise, I told her about what had happened at primary school, and she suggested that perhaps it was a case of 'if you can't beat 'em, join 'em' on Tony's part, and that it might be best to split the group up a bit. In the end, two of the boys were moved to other classes. Although Tony remained friends with the third for a while, he soon moved on to friendships with other boys in his class, and he hasn't been involved in bullying since, either as a bully or on the receiving end. I don't think that he really enjoyed taunting other children – it was more the relief that it wasn't him really.

As Tony's story shows, relationships established in primary school can be shaken up by the admixture of children from other schools, and secondary schools often actively encourage this by separating children from the same school when they make up their first-year classes. This is hardly ever a popular move with the children involved, who would usually rather stay with the people they are used to, even if they don't really like them very much. It can, however, be an opportunity for change for the good. As children mature they can outgrow the friendships they made in primary school, but find it hard to free themselves from the friends they habitually spend most of their time with. A change of school can give them a chance to make the break without having to take the initiative themselves.

The transition from primary to secondary school is undeniably easier, though, if it is made with at least one or two familiar people, even if they don't end up being your child's bosom friends. Although it is difficult to plan this far ahead, it is worth making your choice of primary school, perhaps even playgroup or nursery, on the basis of the secondary school your child will ultimately attend. Of course, house moves and other factors may make this impossible, but it is a point worth considering when you weigh one primary school against another, often with precious little else to choose between them.

Choosing schools

No child will reach her full potential, personally or academically in an environment where she is weighed down by the fear and anxiety bullying arouses in everyone – bully, victim or bystander – who comes into contact with it, so there is little point in basing your choice on exam league tables alone. Schools are often reluctant to publish details of their anti-bullying policies for fear of suggesting to parents that they have a problem with bullying, so the information they give to prospective parents may say very little about the attitudes and policies of the school in this respect, and it is essential that you ask the headteacher or head of first year in person just what is being done to prevent bullying in their school, and to tackle it when it does occur, as it inevitably will from time to time.

Any staff member at the school, and any child for that matter, should be able to tell you exactly what the school's policy is regarding bullying, and what the school does on a regular basis to reinforce that policy. It has been clearly shown that the best way to tackle bullying in schools is to bring it out in the open and keep it there, and to establish a clearly defined procedure for dealing with incidents of bullying when they do occur. If the person you are talking to cannot answer your questions fully and in detail, then there must be some doubt about the existence or effectiveness of an anti-bullying policy within the school.

Beware the following responses (listed with their translations):

- *'We take this problem very seriously. Bullying is punished most severely.'* We don't know how to stop bullying occurring, but by golly when it does we tackle it by doing our level best to frighten the heck out of the bullies, and hope that they won't do it again. What do we do for the victim? Well, isn't that enough?

- *'Fortunately, bullying is not a problem in this school.'* Bullying is not a problem for the staff in this school.

- *'We don't allow bullying.'* We hand each new first year a pamphlet listing the rules of behaviour. We don't see any need to mention bullying again – after all, it might give them ideas.

- *'Of course, all schools get the odd child who just doesn't fit in, but apart from that we haven't had any problems.'* If you get bullied, it's probably your fault, and you're on your own.

Effective measures

Much has been written on the subject of preventing and controlling bullying in schools, but three measures stand out again and again in research findings and observations as being particularly effective:

- *The ethos of the school.* It should be clearly stated and restated at every opportunity, by means of codes of conduct, assemblies, PSE (Personal and Social Education), class discussions and so on, that bullying is not acceptable in this school. Staff must show themselves to be equally committed to this policy: the use of intimidation, humiliation and ridicule by teachers to control children will make nonsense of any anti-bullying policy.

- *Flashpoints.* Care should be taken to pinpoint the danger areas within the school where bullying takes place – a questionnaire for pupils can be helpful in gathering this sort of information. Having identified these danger areas, steps must be taken to provide adequate supervision, or to reorganize school schedules so that large numbers of children do not congregate in these areas, or move around the school from class to class, at any one time.

- *Dealing with incidents of bullying.* If children are to feel confident enough to report bullying incidents, they must know that their report will be listened to, taken seriously and thoroughly investigated. Every staff member should be aware of the school's policy for dealing with complaints of bullying, and all incidents of bullying should be recorded, along with any action taken. All those involved, children, staff and parents, should be informed of the outcome.

Any school which takes bullying seriously should be familiar with the above points, and should be able to tell you how they have implemented them within their school, for instance:

- Assessment of the problem within the school by means of a questionnaire for pupils.
- Established and written policy on bullying, familiar to all staff members and pupils.
- School contract laying down rules of behaviour, contributed to and voted in by pupils, and signed by everyone.
- Regular exposure of the issue in PSE, assemblies, through drama, class discussion, and in other ways.
- Written code of conduct issued to all children on a regular basis.
- Clearly defined procedure for reporting bullying to staff, known to all the children and regularly discussed.
- Involvement of parents in the school's dealings with bullies and victims when an incident has been reported.

- Training in prevention and recognition for staff.
- Special measures to protect new intake from older children, e.g., separate playground or playtimes.
- Timetabling to avoid 'rush-hour' problems, where large numbers of children move around the school at the same time.
- Institution of 'bully courts' (see chapter 7).

If whoever interviews prospective pupils and parents doesn't seem clear about the school's anti-bullying measures, then they are probably not effective. A school which has not thought out and implemented a school-wide policy on bullying is simply not taking the problem seriously enough.

See for yourself

Looking around the school on a special 'prospective pupils' evening' might give you an insight into the organizational and marketing skills of the headteacher and department heads, but it won't give you much of an idea of how it feels to be a pupil there. If you really want to know what the school is like, make an appointment to visit on a normal school day – there should be no objections to this. Take the opportunity to observe the way that children treat each other in the corridors, playground, changing rooms, and anywhere else where they are not directly supervised.

Ask around

If you can, talk to parents who have already got a child at the school you are interested in. For a true 'warts and all' view, though, it's best to talk to the children themselves. If there is bullying, they will know about it.

No school can please all of the pupils (or parents) all of the time, so don't expect unmitigated praise. Your best indication to the quality of the school will be from the sort of complaints parents and pupils have, and how the school has handled problems in the past. If incidents of bullying have been reported and thoroughly and successfully tackled, you may be on to a winner.

Single sex vs. mixed schools – how important is this?

As we saw in chapter 1, bullying is likely to be more of a problem in a single-sex school, but other factors are probably equally important in determining the extent of the problem within an individual school. A single-sex school with a well-defined and rigorously observed policy on bullying may well be a better bet than a mixed school with a haphazard approach or none at all. Try to visit several possible schools, talk to children and parents who know them well, and get a feeling for the ethos of each.

Starting at a new school

Starting a new school is a difficult time for your child, whether he is starting in the reception class, moving between infant and junior or primary and secondary schools, or changing schools as the result of a house move or problems in another school. It is important that your child gets off to a good start, but some factors will make this more difficult for him:

- No pre-school experience of playgroup or nursery.
- No one he knows starting school with him.
- Moving to a secondary school outside the catchment area of his primary school, where he won't know anyone but others are likely to be with groups from their primary schools.
- Joining the school after the first year, when friendships are already established.
- Background of involvement in bullying in a previous school.

There are several ways in which you can help your child to overcome these difficulties.

● *Pre-school experience*

A good playgroup or nursery will help ease your child into school, even if she has only spent one or two terms there, but it isn't essential. The really important thing is that she has plenty of experience of being with children of her own age, and of adapting to different surroundings. Playing at friends' houses will help to achieve both of these. Make sure that you spend plenty of time in the months before she starts talking about school and what will happen there, and take her to visit the school she will be attending if possible.

● *Making friends*

As every child knows, if you've got friends around you, you are much less likely to be picked on by bullies. You can help your child to establish friendships with children he will start school with, and

74

to make friends quickly once he has started. The school itself may be willing to put you in touch with the parents of other new children, but failing this a local playgroup will probably be happy to introduce you to someone who is starting primary school at the same time. Once you've tracked down some potential friends, you can arrange get-togethers – you may even make some new friends yourself this way!

This is relatively easy with the primary-school child, but eleven and twelve-year-olds are often quite unreceptive to their parents' ideas of suitable friendships, and simply inviting someone your child doesn't know from Adam over to tea is likely to meet with a pretty lukewarm reception from both the children concerned. Encouraging your child to become involved in activities where she will meet children of her own age from other schools can help, though. Even if they don't meet anyone who ends up in their first-year class, the social skills and adaptability they will learn from mixing with other children will stand them in good stead. See chapter 4 for suggestions.

If your child has experienced bullying in primary school, and will be moving up to secondary school with the other children involved, it is worth trying to change his relationship with the bullies before the move. Some parents have done this successfully by inviting the bully or bullies to their house and making sure they had a thoroughly good time. This is even more likely to succeed if you can make friends with the bully's parents as well. The children who have bullied your child are less likely to do so if there is some degree of involvement between the families, and may even accept him into their group – but this could involve him in bullying others, as we saw in Tony's story, so you will need to monitor the situation carefully. If he has been drawn into bullying already, the move could give him the chance to break away from the gang. If you can help him to make new friends, either before he starts secondary school or once he is there, it will be that much easier for him to avoid falling in with the same crowd again, or becoming their victim.

• *Changing schools*

Perhaps you have decided to move your child to a new school in order to escape bullying. Unfortunately this doesn't always work, and may even make matters worse. Often the child carries the factors that encouraged bullying, or the lack of confidence and self-esteem that have resulted from her experiences, to her new school with her, with the added disadvantage of joining the school in midstream, when everyone else has already had a chance to settle in. She may need a lot of help to regain her confidence (see chapter 4), and you will need to choose her new school with great care, and make staff aware of the problems she had at her previous school.

When things go wrong

Good preparation and a careful choice of school can minimize your child's chances of becoming involved in bullying, but nothing that you, your child or the school can do can eliminate the possibility altogether. As we have seen in this and earlier chapters, there are many ways in which you can help your child to cope with bullying by:

- feeling good;
- making friends;
- being prepared;
- learning anti-bullying strategies.

When bullying is taking place at school, however, it is vitally important that the headteacher and staff know what is going on, and work with you and your child to stop it, both for your child's sake and that of other children. In the next chapter, we look at how best you can approach the school, and what you can expect them to do to help your child.

7
Helping the school to help your child

If you find that your child is being bullied either in or on the way to and from school, or is being bullied outside school by children he goes to school with, it is essential that you talk to his teacher, class tutor or year head as soon as possible. Most schools will also want to know about any 'inter-school' bullying that might be taking place when children from different schools meet. The school should, and in most cases will, be concerned to deal effectively with this sort of trouble as quickly as possible, before it becomes entrenched.

You will undoubtedly be feeling very upset and probably very angry too, but try to resist the urge to blame the school out of hand for failing to protect your child. Bullying will happen sometimes in even the best-regulated of schools, and the 'proof of the pudding' is in how the school handles these incidents when they arise. Take a little time to compose yourself, then make an appointment; you should be offered one the same day if you ring early and say it's urgent.

Who should I talk to, and what should I say?

Your first point of contact is your child's form teacher. She will usually know your child, and often the other children involved as well, and is in the best position to assess the situation and suggest remedies, although this may not be the case in secondary school, where class tutors sometimes only see their classes for registration, and may not teach them at all.

A general chat about your child may be helpful, but don't lose sight of the reason for your visit: to report the bullying and get something done to stop it. Whatever else you cover, you will need to ask your child's form teacher to:

- investigate your child's complaints;
- keep you informed of the results;
- inform the headteacher of your meeting.

It may be that your child's teacher is able to pinpoint factors that are contributing to his problems. Occasionally a child has a particularly annoying habit which makes it hard for other children to tolerate him, or is just socially inept in some way. You need to know if this is the case, so that you can help your child to change; but it isn't an excuse for bullying, and doesn't alter the purpose of your visit, which is to get the bullying stopped.

Get your facts straight

It is important that you go along to the interview with your child's teacher armed with as much information as possible. Don't rely on your memory; write down all the facts you have gathered so far and all the questions you want to ask, or you are certain to miss something out. From the first moment you suspect that bullying may be a problem, either you or your child should keep a detailed diary of events, including:

- names of any children involved, including witnesses;
- dates and times of incidents;
- where the incidents took place;
- details of injuries and any treatment received for them;
- details of damage to or theft of property.

It is also advisable that you keep a record of your dealings with the school:

- dates of meetings and who they were with;
- main points covered;
- copies of letters sent and received.

After each meeting, write to those involved confirming the main points covered and detailing any action agreed upon. Send a copy to the headteacher and, in secondary school, to your child's year head. This may sound a lot of work, and of course if all goes well you may never need to refer to your records again, but it is useful to have a written record of any action the school agreed to take, which you can refer to if things don't get done. If you should need to take your complaint further – to the school governors or the education authority, for instance – this written evidence will be invaluable in backing up your case with hard fact.

What can I expect the school to do?

● *Take the matter seriously*

Don't be fobbed off with excuses, or attempts to shift the blame on to your child: 'Boys will be boys, your child is being over-sensitive', 'no one else has complained of bullying'. Whatever the cause, bullying is not acceptable, and the school should take every possible step to see that it doesn't happen again.

● *Protect your child until the matter can be sorted out*

Having spoken to your child's form teacher, you can expect that action will be taken straight away to protect your child from further bullying, so that she can continue to go to school without fear of further attacks. However committed the school is to sorting out bullying problems, it will take them time to talk to all the children and parents involved, and to decide on a course of action, but once they are aware of the situation it should be possible for the school to arrange increased supervision or a safe place for your child to go during breaks and lunch hours.

● *Talk to the victim, the bully and witnesses*

The first step in any investigation the school undertakes is to hear both sides of the story, and this means talking to everyone involved, both your child and the child or children who have been bullying her. This doesn't mean that they don't believe your child's story, but it is important for everyone in the school that incidents of bullying are seen to be fairly and fully investigated, and that everyone's point of view is listened to. How would you feel if someone accused your child of bullying, and she was punished out of hand, without the chance to give her account of events?

If your child has been bullied often, other children are sure to know about it, but they may need encouragement to talk to staff about what they know. This will be easier in a school with an established anti-bullying policy, but in any case children should be offered the chance to talk to a teacher in confidence about what they have seen. If your child knows the names of children who have witnessed the bullying, they should be passed on to the investigating teacher.

● *Talk to parents*

The parents of both the bully and the bullied child should be brought into any investigation of bullying from the earliest stages. Parents, and not the school, are ultimately responsible for the behaviour of their child. Having seen both sets of parents, and agreed with them upon a course of action, the school should then keep all concerned informed about the outcome of the investigation and any action proposed or taken.

● *Take action to prevent further bullying*

Having investigated your child's allegations of bullying, and established the identity of those responsible, the school will need to take active measures to ensure that the bully or bullies take the consequences of their actions, and are prevented from further bullying. There are several courses of action open to them.

Measures the school can take after an incident

● *Making amends*

The first and most important step that the school can take is to see that the bully makes amends to his victim. Making amends helps bullies face up to their responsibility for making another individual suffer, but also and equally importantly helps victims over their distress; it puts the blame squarely where it should be – on the bully. Some ways in which bullies can make amends are suggested in chapter 5.

● *Punishment*

In less serious cases of bullying, making amends may be enough to prevent the bully from repeating her behaviour. In serious or persistent cases, however, the school may decide to punish the bully, both for her disruptive behaviour and for the staff time she has wasted in the investigation that followed. Schools will have their own punishments, such as writing lines, detentions, being put 'on report', etc. Whatever punishment is decided on, you and your child should be kept informed of the outcome.

● *On-site suspension*

Some schools operate an on-site suspension system. The bully who is suspended on-site goes to school in the normal way, but either works alone and is kept away from other children at break and lunch times, or takes part in classes but is not allowed to mix with other children other than in a classroom setting: kept in at lunch and break times, let out of school after other children have left for home, and so on. In effect, the bully is getting the worst of both worlds – all the work of school without any of the compensating social life. This can be a most effective punishment, and brings home to the bully the principle that being part of a group means abiding by its rules. It also helps the victim by removing the bully from the situations in which the bullying is likely to have taken place.

● *Exclusion*
The school may decide to exclude the bully from school completely, allowing her back only after a suitable period and following a formal interview with her and her parents, in which she must show that her attitude has changed. Having a child at home all day in school time can be a big inconvenience for parents, who may bring considerable pressure to bear on their child to change her ways.

Where there has been persistent bullying, the school may consider excluding the child permanently. This really is a last resort, as the reasons for her exclusion will go on record, and she may find it very difficult to find a new school. Most schools will prefer to do all they can to help the bully change her ways before making the decision to exclude her permanently.

● *Bully courts*
Schools with a persistent bullying problem may decide to establish 'bully courts.' Pioneered by Kidscape, the bully court consists of a panel of children, some elected by their peers and some nominated by teachers, with a teacher as an adviser.

Any complaint of bullying comes before the bully court, and everyone involved, including witnesses, is summoned to put forward their side of the story. Having heard everyone's submission, the court arrives at a conclusion about the incident and, if they feel it is justified, suggests a punishment for the bully. The bully then has the option of accepting this punishment, or appealing to the headteacher.

This system has been proven most effective in reducing the incidence of bullying in schools, but it does need to be used very carefully if it is not to become a tool for revenge, or itself just another form of insitutionalized bullying. Bully courts will only work in schools with a strong, established, anti-bullying policy, where every child feels responsible for ending bullying within their school community, even if they are involved only as a bystander. If your school doesn't have a bully court and bullying is a persistent problem, why not suggest that they institute one, with help from Kidscape (address on page 111)?

He doesn't want to tell

If your child has talked freely to you about the problem, you will be able to ask him for details, although he may be reluctant to give names. Often, though, parents will have found out about bullying in a more roundabout way, perhaps from another child or parent, or suspect that their child is being bullied but have no concrete proof. In these cases, you may be unable to provide much in the way of evidence to back up your concerns. Don't be put off by the school saying that it is impossible for them to take action without evidence. Names and details make investigation easier, of course, but even if it proves impossible for the school to track down the culprits in this particular incident, there is much that they can do to discourage bullying generally; even a general warning to the whole school, if made with sufficient conviction and carried through, can be very effective.

If you feel that it would be wrong or damaging for your child to be approached directly, or if you don't want her to know that you have approached the school, there are other ways in which investigations can be made.

- Every child in the class can be interviewed. The tutor only needs to tell them that some bullying has been reported – no names need be mentioned, and since everyone has been called in, your child will not be identified as the source of the information, even to herself.

- If the bullies have been identified, they can simply be told that they have been seen bullying other children. Since they are unlikely to have confined their bullying activities to your child alone, even if they do work out that they must have been shopped by a victim, they will not be able to pin it on any one child with any certainty.

Helping the victim

In the rush to find and punish the bully, the needs of the victim can sometimes be forgotten. It isn't enough simply that the bullying is stopped; the child who has suffered needs help in regaining confidence, and reassurance that he was not to blame for what happened. The making of amends by the bully – perhaps in the form of a public apology – will go a long way towards this, but the victim's problems may not end there. The process of investigation and reconciliation of a bullying incident should include some counselling for the victim, perhaps by the class teacher or another teacher appointed for the purpose, in which he is reassured that he is not the only one to have suffered in this way, that it could happen to anyone at any time, and that the responsibility rests squarely with the bully. The situation should then be carefully monitored, and the victim should be seen again at regular intervals, until there is clearly no further need for support.

Support groups

It is much easier for both victims and bullies to get help if there is an established mechanism within the school for doing so. To this end, some schools have instituted support groups, run jointly by teachers and social workers or counsellors, to help children cope with the pressures of bullying. If your child's school hasn't got a support group, why not suggest that they form one?

Putting the pressure on

In a perfect world, a report of bullying would always result in swift and effective action on the part of the school. Unfortunately, bullying has only recently been acknowledged as a problem at all, and not all schools have yet established a policy for dealing with incidents. Even in schools where bullying is taken seriously, there may still be members of staff who don't see it as a particular problem, or who just don't recognize it at all. If a complaint of bullying to your child's form teacher is brushed aside as unimportant, if the school blames your child for provoking the bullying, or if action is promised but doesn't seem to materialize, what should you do?

- Take your complaint further up the school – to the year head or headteacher.

- Ask a parent representative on the Parent Teacher Association to raise the matter at PTA meetings and report back to you on the result. As always, it is best to put your request in writing, along with all the evidence you have collected and details of your dealings with the school so far.

- Contact the Board of Governors (called the School Board in Scotland). They are legally bound to listen to your complaint and take any action necessary within the law. If you don't know how to contact any of the governors, you can get their names, addresses and telephone numbers from the school, which is obliged to give them to you.

- Bring in the police. You are legally entitled to do this, whether the school agrees or not, although it will help if the school co-operates with their enquiries. Given the choice, most schools will prefer to handle bullying problems themselves, and knowing that you are willing to involve the law may encourage them to take effective action. For information on how to get police help and what sort of reception you can expect, see chapter 10.

Longer-term measures

As well as investigating your immediate complaint, where a school has a bullying problem, individuals, or preferably a group of parents, can ask the Board of Governors to initiate the following measures:

- anti-bullying policy as outlined in chapter;
- support groups run by teachers and social workers/counsellors;
- bully courts
- involvement of parents by means of a letter asking them to explain the seriousness of bullying to their children;
- meetings bringing parents and children into school together to talk about bullying.

If your child is the bully

The victim's parents, whilst shocked and angry at finding that their child has been bullied, can at least reasonably expect that the school will be on their side. How much worse, then, to be called into school to find that your own child has been accused of being a bully? The feelings of the parent in this situation may be very much like those of the victim's parents. Why are they picking on my child? How can I protect her? Hard though it is for most of us to believe that our child has done anything seriously wrong, it is important to acknowledge that we really don't know everything about them, and the way they behave outside the home, and to listen to the evidence with an open mind before reaching any conclusions.

An effective school anti-bullying policy will protect the child who is accused of bullying as well as the victim. If an accusation has been made, he is entitled to expect a fair hearing, and his parents are entitled to be kept informed of its progress and outcome.

You may have reported that your child is being bullied, and been told, after investigation, that she is herself accused of bullying. Research has shown that persistent bullies often think of themselves as being victimized or picked on by other children, so don't dismiss such findings out of hand – perhaps she really does need help with feelings of inadequacy or fear, and to find better ways of handling them. If the school cites your child's attitude or behaviour as a cause of the problem, or asserts that she is in fact bullying or taunting other children and that what she reports to you as bullying is simply their reaction to her behaviour, and you disagree with their assertions, you can ask for a school-based assessment of your child by an educational psychologist.

What if the bully's a teacher?

Some teachers still use fear, taunts and humiliation to control their classes. Sometimes a teacher will take a dislike to a particular child, and belittle everything he does, labelling him lazy, badly behaved, or just plain thick. Because children and parents expect teachers to use their authority responsibly, this form of bullying may not be recognized as such, although it is potentially extremely damaging to the child.

If you suspect that your child is being bullied by a particular teacher, perhaps because she has complained to you about it, because she is obviously distressed before or after a particular class, or because you have heard about it from other children or parents, the best approach in the first instance is probably to talk to the teacher concerned. Don't accuse her of bullying your child, simply say that you are concerned about how she is getting on and want to ask the teacher's advice. The response may help you to gauge her attitude to your child.

If a teacher is bullying your child or others, the situation must be brought to the attention of the school. Often, teachers will be aware of a colleague's methods, but it takes complaints by children and parents to get anything done. A good school will listen to your worries and take action; in the secondary school attended by my own children, a teacher was sacked after complaints from parents, and the reason for his dismissal made known to the children. This went a long way toward reversing the damage he had done to some individuals, and increasing the children's confidence in the fairness and sincerity of the school's anti-bullying policy.

Should we keep our child away from school?

If your child is being bullied at school, your instinct will probably be to keep her at home. Most schools will advise against this, rightly asserting that the longer she stays away, the more difficult it will be for her to return. This is all well and good if they can assure you that your child will be protected from bullying while at school and as she arrives and leaves. If they can't, or if promises of protection are not fulfilled, then your own instincts are probably your best guide. There is absolutely no point in forcing a distressed and frightened child back into school for another day of fear and anticipation; she will learn nothing and the damage caused by the bullying will get steadily more difficult to reverse.

Most schools will take any complaint of bullying seriously, and take action to investigate and resolve the problem. Having reported an incident of bullying to your child's school, it is important that you give them a fair chance to sort things out, and in most cases they will do so successfully. Sometimes the school's attempts to protect an individual child from victimization will fail, perhaps because lack of an effective anti-bullying policy has allowed the problem to run out of control, because there is a weak link in the chain of commitment needed from all the staff concerned, or simply because the child concerned has been so damaged by bullying that he can't escape from the role of victim. Bullying is not just bad behaviour, it can be and often is a criminal offence. Your child is entitled to the protection of the law, in or out of school, and in the chapter that follows we look at what the police can do to help in the battle against bullying.

8

Bullying and the law

In cases of serious school bullying the school itself may decide to call in the police. In practice, however, many schools are reluctant to involve the police in what they see as an internal discipline problem. The reputation of a school is not enhanced by reports of police intervention, and everyone concerned, parents and school alike, feels reluctant to involve children in a criminal investigation if there is any alternative. Bullying can, and often does, involve a criminal offence, however, and if you feel that your child needs the protection of the law you are entitled to call in the police, whether the school agrees to their involvement or not.

When bullying takes place outside school, and where approaching the bully or her parents has failed or where bullies cannot be identified, the victim's only recourse may be the law. Parents may hesitate to ask for help, however, because they doubt that their complaints of bullying will be taken seriously, or feel that the police are powerless to act anyway where minors are involved. So when, if ever, should parents involve the police in cases of bullying, and what can they do to help?

When is bullying a crime?

Bullying itself is not a criminal offence. There are no police statistics concerning bullying and no specific police policy for dealing with complaints. Within the force, though, bullying is recognized as a problem, rather as domestic violence was before specific procedures and legislation were introduced to deal with it, and in some areas special police patrols operate to protect children from gangs of bullies on their way to and from school.

Although bullying itself is not recognized as a criminal offence, the actions of the bully may well constitute a crime. In all the following examples, the actions of the bully could be classified as assault under the Offences Against the Person Act of 1861, and therefore justify prosecution.

Matthew was leaving the local sports centre when he was stopped by a group of boys, who asked him what school he went to. His answer didn't please them, and they pushed him around, punching him in the face and causing a black eye and bloody nose.

David was taking a short cut back from the shops when a boy he didn't know grabbed him and told him to hand over the new trainers he had bought. He broke free and ran away, colliding with a passing cyclist and breaking his arm.

In both cases, the injuries suffered were a direct or indirect result of the actions of the culprits, and could justify prosecution for actual bodily harm or wounding. There doesn't have to be a physical injury for an offence to have taken place, however.

Tamina was persistently picked on in the playground and on the way to and from school by a group of girls who called her names and told her to 'go back where she came from'. They said they had a knife, and threatened to scar her for life if they saw her again. She became so frightened that she refused to go to school.

Lee sent notes to a boy in his class, whom he suspected of liking his girlfriend, telling him that he was going to catch him on his way home from school one day and break his nose if he saw him talking to her again.

Two boys were caught by the school caretaker in the act of disabling the brakes on a bicycle belonging to another, knowing that he would ride it down a steep hill on his way home from school.

The actions of these bullies could all constitute assault, which is legally defined as:

1. The intentional application of force to the person of another without his consent, or the threat of such force by act or gesture.
2. Any act which constitutes any attempt, offer or threat to use violence or any unlawful force to the person of another.

Injury to another persons's state of mind – a frequent result of persistent bullying – may also constitute an assault. Tamina became so frightened that she refused to go to school and, backed by medical evidence, this might be sufficient to justify prosecution.

Bullying doesn't always result in injury, physical or mental. It can also involve theft, robbery or extortion. Some bullies steal dinner money from other children on a regular basis, others take or destroy possessions. These actions are as illegal in school as they are outside, although most schools would appreciate the chance to discipline the culprit themselves rather than become involved in an inconvenient and disruptive police investigation.

Will they prosecute?

The law treats children differently from adults, and the extent to which children can be held legally responsible and accountable for their actions varies with age. Anyone under seventeen years is legally defined as a juvenile, and within this category children are further divided into three distinct age groups for the purposes of prosecution and sentencing.

- *Under ten*. A child under ten years old cannot be found guilty of any criminal offence, and is immune from prosecution. If a child in this age group persistently breaks the law, however, he may be taken into local authority care.

- *ten to under fourteen*. A child in this age group can be tried and found guilty of a criminal offence, although it must be shown that she knew she was doing wrong. Whilst the child can be found guilty of most of the same offences as an adult, she will be tried in a juvenile court, and the penalties imposed by the court will be different – usually involving restrictions on where she lives and how she behaves, enforced attendance at school, and regular supervision and counselling.

- *fourteen to under seventeen*. Whilst still classified as a juvenile, a child in this age group is expected to take responsibility for any criminal act he performs; it is no longer a defence to show that he didn't know that he was breaking the law. If prosecuted, he will still be tried in a juvenile court, but may now be sentenced to detention in a young offender's institution if the seriousness of his offence is thought to merit a custodial sentence.

Although it might be quite clear that a bully is behaving illegally, the stumbling block as far as securing a prosecution goes is often the difficulty in finding witnesses to the bullying. Often the only ones to have seen what happened will be other children, whose evidence may not be strong enough to make a good legal case. Without witnesses, any prosecution will fail, and the police may be unwilling to waste their time, as they see it, on cases where a conviction cannot be secured.

Even where a criminal offence has clearly been committed, the police have a good deal of discretion in deciding whether or not a prosecution should be brought. If a juvenile admits guilt they can decide to caution her instead of proceeding with a prosecution. This is not the same as just giving the child an informal talking-to, which an officer investigating an incident of bullying may decide to do whether anyone admits guilt or not. Whilst an official caution issued to a juvenile does not go on to a criminal record, it is noted and can be referred to if the child appears before a juvenile or criminal court in the future.

Detection and prosecution of offenders is not the only help that the police force has to offer in the fight against bullying, however. Crime prevention is also a major concern of the police force as a whole, and the importance of giving children the right messages about what society and the law expects of them is acknowledged by the police force as a whole, not least in the appointment of schools liaison officers – serving police officers who visit schools on a regular basis to talk to children about personal safety, crime prevention and becoming good citizens.

Schools liaison work has undergone a radical change in the last ten years, and officers are now trained to use activities and group discussion to get their point across; most will now see children in class groups rather than an assembly. WPC Laura Green, a bright, extrovert young woman in her twenties, is one of the new breed of schools liaison officers; in the past they have tended to be older policemen, looking for an easier option towards the end of their career. Talking to children about bullying is very much a part of her brief, and she explains the role that the police have to play both in preventing its occurrence and in dealing with incidents when they occur. Laura rejects the authoritarian approach favoured by many of the old school of liaison officers.

My job is to reduce juvenile crime by explaining what it is – ultimately to make them better citizens. Part of that job involves explaining to children who may have had the wrong examples at home what is and is not acceptable behaviour in the eyes of our society. It's a difficult area, of course, and the last thing I want is to tell children that what their parents have told them is wrong, but I can point out that threatening or physically assaulting anyone, even your own child, is a criminal offence. I encourage the children to call me by my first name, and I make it clear that I am not there just to tell them about crime, but to help the victim as well. I hope that they would feel able to talk to me if they had a problem, and I would certainly listen and try to help them sort it out, even if no criminal act was involved.

If bullying is taking place outside school, or if approaches to the school have failed to bring about an improvement in the situation, the victims and their parents are entitled to help from the police. Even if there are no witnesses to the incident, I would like to think that an officer would still take the complaint seriously, perhaps seeing all the children involved and making it clear to the bullies that their behaviour is not acceptable. Unfortunately, the prime concern of the police has to be in securing convictions. A complaint about bullying is unlikely to lead to a successful prosecution in most cases, which means a lot of time and hassle for the officers involved with no impact on the crime figures. For this reason, some officers may be less sympathetic than they might be to a complaint of this sort.

You are, however, within your rights in asking the police to take action, though you may need to persevere. Don't give up if the first officer you contact is reluctant to take any action; ask to speak to another. WPC Laura Green suggests that you make contact with the schools liaison officer if you feel that you are not getting anywhere with your complaint.

Unfortunately, we do tend to become a bit cynical in this job. When you are sent out to your hundredth burglary, you sometimes have to make a real effort to remember that it is probably the first time it has ever happened to these people, and for them it is an overwhelming and devastating event. Unless the officer involved has had personal experience of bullying, either in their own childhood or through one of their own children, it can be hard for them to understand how terrible it can be for the victim, even if the incident has fallen short of a criminal offence.

If you are unlucky the first time you complain, don't give up –

keep going until you find someone who will help. A schools liaison officer will usually have an understanding of how children might feel in these circumstances, and may well know the children concerned, victim and bully, as well as having a relationship with the school, which can help if the bullying is taking place there.

Unfortunately, not all schools welcome the schools liaison officer's approaches. The head of a local authority school, whilst under no compulsion to allow access to pupils, will have to justify himself to the school's board of governors if visits are not allowed. The heads of private schools are under no such constraint, and often feel that visits from the schools liaison officer are not appropriate for their pupils. Parents can exert their influence here, on both governors and headteachers, to ensure that schools liaison officers are allowed into their schools on a regular basis, for the benefit and protection of their children.

Often, children are reluctant to ask for help because they are not sure that they will be taken seriously. Schools liaison officers can help to reinforce the message that threatening, intimidating or hurting people is wrong, and that the culprit will be punished. As always, it is vitally important that this message is backed up with action, and that all the children involved see that a complaint, once made, will be pursued to its conclusion. If you do complain to the police, it is important that you persist with your complaint, even if you don't seem to be getting anywhere initially. The police force as a whole does take this problem seriously, after all, statistics show that some 68 per cent of all chronic school bullies become violent adults with a history of criminal offences.

Antony Benn, a Metropolitan policeman for twenty-nine years, and in charge of community crime prevention at New Scotland Yard for two of these, has this to say on the subject of bullying, in *Bullying: a practical guide for schools*:

> Bullying in all its forms is pernicious, and needs rooting out at the earliest opportunity. Police intervention with rigorous investigation may be the answer in the worst of cases, and I would urge the reporting to the Police of any incidents of violent bullying before the matter escalates.

9

Educating your child
at home

For some of the victims of school bullying, it may simply be too late
to put things right. School will have become a place of such
inescapable misery for them that they cannot face returning to it day
after day. If they are forced back into the classroom, they will be
incapable of fulfilling their academic potential, weighed down as
they are with fear and anxiety. Rather than see their child battle
daily against her fears, with all the damage to confidence, behaviour
problems and disruption to family life that entails, some parents will
decide to educate their child at home.

Is home education an option?

The law does not oblige you to send your child to school. It simply
states that he must be educated, and that it is the parents'
responsibility to see that he is. This is clearly established in sections
36 and 76 of the 1944 Education Act:

Section 36
It shall be the duty of the parent of every child of compulsory
school age to cause him to receive efficient full-time education
suitable to his age, ability and aptitude and to any special
educational needs he may have, either by regular attendance at
school or otherwise.

Section 76
In the exercise and performance of all powers and duties
conferred and imposed on them by this act the Minister and
Local Authorities shall have regard to the general principal that,
so far as is compatible with the provisions of suitable public
expenditure, pupils are to be educated in accordance with the
wishes of their parents.

The Northern Ireland Act of 1947 contains sections identical to
these, while the Scottish Education Act of 1962 contains similar
sections.

93

The rights of parents to determine the sort of education their child receives are further upheld in Article 26 of the United Nations Declaration of Human Rights, which states that 'parents shall have a prior right to choose the kind of education that shall be given to their children', and in the Protocol to the European Convention for the Protection of Human Rights and Fundamental Freedoms, Article, 2, March 1952: 'No person shall be denied the right to education. In the exercise of any function which it assumes in relation to education and to teaching, the state shall respect the right of parents to ensure such education and teaching is in conformity with their own religious and philosophical convictions.'

Help for parents

Education Otherwise, a self-help organization formed by a group of parents in the 1970s, offers support, advice and information to families interested in or practising home-based education as an alternative to schooling for their children. EO's members have found that Local Education Authority officials, who have a duty to ensure that an 'efficient' and 'suitable' education is being provided for any child not attending school, are usually sympathetic and co-operative in their dealings with parents who have decided to educate their children at home. In the event of a serious dispute arising, however, the LEA may pass the matter on to the magistrate's court, so it is advisable for any parent contemplating educating a child at home to contact either EO or the Children's Home-Based Education Association (see page 111 for details) for advice on presenting their case to the LEA. Once a child is engaged in home education, the LEA will send an inspector to monitor her progress from time to time.

Membership of EO is on the increase. Although many people join without giving a reason, Jane Lowe of EO believes that bullying is often the reason for people taking their children away from school and educating them at home. She stresses that you don't have to be a teacher to educate your child – in fact the majority of home educators have no formal qualifications. You don't have to work to a timetable, and you are not obliged to follow the National Curriculum, although you may do so if you wish. Neither is choosing to educate your child at home necessarily a once-and-for-all decision:

Sometimes a period at home can give the child a chance to regain self-esteem and self-confidence, and then go back into school again. Changing schools can be fruitless if the problems that caused the child to become a victim remain unchanged, and we have seen cases where children have moved from school to school, even area to area, in an attempt to escape bullying, but the problem has recurred again and again. A time in home education can break this tragic continuum, and give them a chance to get back into the swing of things again with renewed confidence and hope.

Case history

In principle, then, home education appears to be a sound alternative for the child whose experience of school has been tainted by bullying. For most of us, though, school and childhood are inseparable; we might think that educating our child at home sounds a good idea, but find it impossible to imagine how it works in practice. Anthony's story, below, gives us an insight into the sort of problems that can lead parents to withdraw their child from school, and what that decision means in terms of day-to-day family life.

Anthony's story

Anthony is now eleven and a half. His parents took him out of his state primary school eighteen months ago, and he and his mother are actively involved in their local Home Education group. His mother, Vicky, tells his story.

Anthony spent six years in the school system, and from day one he was ill at ease. He had difficulty making and keeping friends, although this had not been the case at playgroup or nursery, but the worst problem was with his schoolwork. His teachers reported that he was uncooperative, and got little work done, although they acknowledged that he was a bright child, and what work he did was certainly up to standard.

We had a move of house, and he changed schools, but the problems continued. It wasn't specifically bullying at this stage, but he still didn't seem to make any lasting friendships, he would come out of school tense and 'hyped up' and his teachers continued to report underachievement and reluctance to work.

We worried more and more about his lack of academic achievement – no one denied that he was a bright child, and should have been doing better – and in his second year in the juniors we moved him to a school with a reputation for academic achievement, in the hope that he would find the atmosphere more stimulating and get down to work at last. It turned out to be a disastrous move. After his first day there I was told that there had been a problem with another boy, but he had handled it well and it had blown over. Two days later, he was swung around by his coat sleeve in the playground and flung to the ground, grazing his mouth. Within six months Anthony was suffering continuous physical and verbal abuse. There was a particular group of three or four boys in his class that the school just couldn't seem to handle. Anthony was just a bit different – he was tall for his age, didn't have a strong local accent like most of the other children, and he preferred to play with children younger than himself, which apparently wasn't encouraged at this school.

On one occasion, he was invited to the birthday outing of one of the boys who was bullying him. I was a bit dubious about this, but Anthony wanted to go, so I agreed that he could. When I picked him up after the outing, the father of the birthday boy told me that Anthony had had a miserable time – they had been to the zoo, and he had been kicked and punched all day by the other boys. His words were 'He's just a bit different from the others, isn't he? He's cleverer than them.' On another occasion, a friend picked him up from school for me, and was horrified to be followed home by this same group of boys, shouting rude comments and taunts.

One solution suggested by the headmistress was to move Anthony to another class, to 'give him a break' from the bullies. Since it was only a small school, with one class for each age group, this meant moving him up into an older group, which they did for a short period. The children in his own class assumed that he'd been moved because he'd done something wrong, and of course this compounded his problems. He did start friendships with a few of the children in his class, but it became apparent that they were being warned off by the dominant group – the bullies who were picking on Anthony.

I talked to the school about all this from the outset, but the attitude of his teacher and the headmistress was that Anthony

96

was attracting attention from the bullies, and that he should try to change his behaviour. On one occasion, Anthony was attacked by two boys on his way to the school car park, where he was meeting me after school, and defended himself with an umbrella he was carrying. This incident was seen by two other mothers, who confirmed Anthony's story. We went straight to the headteacher, who summoned the boys to her office there and then. They admitted to having goaded Anthony all day for no reason, and attacking him from behind, and were sent home. The headteacher then sat Anthony down and explained to him at length that he shouldn't have 'over-reacted' to the situation and used his umbrella. She told me later that she had called in the parents of the two boys involved over similar incidents on several other occasions, and it hadn't done any good, so she hadn't thought it worth calling them in again!

In the end, Anthony was frightened to be in any area of the school which wasn't supervised – his teacher said that she would make sure she was around after school when the children were getting ready to go home, as this was a time when he was often picked on, and she was for a while. After a time, though, even this tailed off – I suppose she had other things to do. Anthony's personality was changing – he was becoming verbally aggressive at home and towards other children. He was desperately sensitive – the smallest setback or problem would send him into floods of tears. It began to seem as though his problems at school were our family's sole topic of conversation. I went through a phase of wondering whether I was just being an oversensitive mother, whether perhaps we should encourage him to stand on his own two feet, as some people advised us. Then I was ill for a while, and my father took over the job of collecting Anthony from school. After a few days, he sat us both down and said, 'No child should have to go through this'. Anthony would literally run out of school to meet him, and if he walked into the cloakrooms before he had got out, he would hear other children saying: 'Look out, his grandfather's coming!' It was obvious what had been going on.

Strangely enough, Anthony had never refused to go to school, or pretended to be ill, although every day was obviously an ordeal. One weekend, though, it all came to a head. He was behaving very badly, being rude and unco-operative as he often was in those days, and I finally asked him, in exasperation, just what was really wrong. He broke down and begged not to be sent back to school.

We just didn't know what to do. It was obvious that the situation was unbearable for him, and we knew we just couldn't force him back into it any longer. In desperation, we decided to take him out of school permanently – we didn't even know if it was legal at that stage – and educate him at home.

One thing that really disappointed me was the attitude of Anthony's headmistress. I wrote to her, explaining our decision to remove him from school, and asking her to take the necessary steps to de-register him. A couple of weeks later, we got a letter back from her saying that she had consulted with other members of staff, and their considered opinion was that we were not acting in his best interests. She felt that it was wrong to isolate him, and would be telling the authorities all this in her official recommendations. We were really hurt that she had obviously spent some time considering her reply, and consulting other members of staff, but hadn't taken the trouble to ask us what we intended to do for Anthony. She knew how unhappy he had been at school and, as I pointed out in my reply, it was hardly possible to be more isolated at home or anywhere else than he had been there.

I must admit that the first six months were very difficult. I went about it in totally the wrong way. The only sort of education I knew about was the sort you get at school, where you sit at a desk and get taught things. I was worried about having the right things on paper to show the authorities, to prove that he was having a 'proper education', and I set about this by, in effect, bringing school into my home. Anthony reacted just as I should have expected, with the same uncooperative attitude that had so maddened his teachers at school. I had been at work part time while Anthony was at school, so I had given that up to educate him at home. I wasn't sure that I could face spending all day at home with my child anyway, and his attitude really made me mad. I felt, 'I've given all this up for your benefit, and this is how you repay me!' In time, though, I learned to have faith in Anthony, and to step back a bit. Now I act as a resource rather than a teacher. I advise, guide, put information in front of Anthony and perhaps ask a few questions. If he shows an interest in something we follow it up, if it doesn't seem to catch his imagination we leave it for another time. There are some things I insist on his doing, of course, like basic maths and literacy, but most of the things we study arise naturally out of his interests and the questions any normal child asks about his environment. Recently, for example, he asked why some countries have hurricanes and others don't, and this led to a project on weather and climate. His father is a self-employed landscape gardener, and Anthony sometimes helps him at work – he's learned a lot that way. He helps me at home, too, and he cooks the main meal for all the family once a week. It seems to me that he's getting a much better education for real life than he would have done in the unavoidably narrow environment he would have had at school.

The main worries of any parent contemplating educating their child at home must be firstly that their child will never learn to socialize, and secondly that it will cost them a lot of money. Vicky has not found either to be a problem:

We are very involved with the local Home Education group, which organizes no end of activities for the children. Anthony has no problem at all in socializing with other children of all ages, in fact I have noticed that the children in our Home Education group are far more socially adept than the average school child of their age. Perhaps it's because they mix with such a vast range of people – far more than the child who is at school six hours a day. Our children's education goes on all the time, and we use all the resources we can find to help them. This involves making all sorts of visits and meeting all sorts of people, of all ages and in all walks of life.

Educating your child at home needn't be expensive. Of course, you can spend as much money on it as you want to, but I know several parents who are educating their children on Income Support – I'm not saying that they find it easy, but it certainly can be done. When I worked out what educating Anthony at home was costing us, and compared it with all the costs of a school education – uniform, transport and all the hidden expenses like sponsorship, outings and so on – I found that they worked out about the same. That doesn't take into account the loss of my earnings, of course, but then many mothers are at home with other children anyway, so this won't be a factor for everyone. Anyway, what could be more important than the education and happiness of your child?

Anthony is a normal 11½-year-old. He greases his hair down and uses stick-on tattoos and does all the things that other boys of his age do. The difference is that he does them because he wants to, not because he will be rejected by his peers if he doesn't. He knows that whether or not he ever goes back to school is his choice – no one will force him into that situation ever again – and at the moment he is quite adamant that he doesn't want to. Exams aren't really a problem. At fourteen, he will be legally entitled to apply to a college of further education for an exam course if that is what he wants, or he could take exams by correspondence course. I believe that home education encourages the ability to adapt, to be flexible, and I am convinced that this will be one of his greatest strengths in adult life, particularly in a world where good exam results no longer guarantee anyone a job.

There is no doubt that, for most people, home education is very different from school. Learning is not something reserved for the period between 9 a.m. and 3.30 p.m. on weekdays, but part of everything the child does. Home-educated children mix with a far broader range of people, and gain a breadth of experience unavailable to those undergoing a school education. If your child is unhappy at school, and you are willing to make the commitment in terms of time and effort that educating your child at home requires, the possible benefits for both parent and child make this an option well worth considering.

10

Learning to defend yourself

A few years ago, a father whose son complained of bullying would have been advised to teach the lad to box. This wasn't such a bad idea, not because laying the bully out with a right hook is necessarily the best way to tackle the problem, but because anything that gives a child the chance to develop and achieve, and involves the interest and concern of a parent is likely to bolster his confidence, and so make him a less rewarding target for the bully. The bully himself might also have benefited from a spell at the boxing club, learning to control his aggression and express it in less damaging ways, and gaining confidence from acquiring a skill.

Martial arts

Boxing is not as popular as it used to be, principally because of concerns over the involvement of children in a full-contact combat sport, with all the risk of injury that involves. The modern equivalent of the boxing club, and equally suitable for both girls and boys, is the martial arts class. Most towns now have a karate or judo club, and in many areas the choice is much wider, offering lesser-known disciplines such as tae kwon do and kung-fu. Well taught, these activities can help boost confidence. They may eventually provide your child with physical skills which, in the last resort, she could use in self-defence, but this is probably a far less important consideration, and requires long-term commitment and regular practise. What she really needs, anyway, is a way to avoid or stop fitting into the role of victim, rather than the ability to punch her way out of it.

What a good martial arts class will *not* do, contrary to popular misconception, is make a child behave aggressively. In fact, the reverse is true: martial arts classes are highly disciplined and provide an outlet for the pupil's natural aggression within strictly controlled limits. The child who is having problems handling his aggressive feelings can really benefit from the self-control he will learn at such a class, although he may find it hard going at first and need a lot of encouragement to persevere.

Choosing a martial arts class can be confusing. The list below is by no means exhaustive, but does describe the most commonly practised martial arts. There are others, but many of them are just variations on these themes.

Ju-jitsu

Ju-jitsu is the oldest of the Japanese fighting arts, from which most of the more modern and specialized disciplines were developed. Throwing, holding, striking, kicking and joint-locking techniques are all utilized, along with anything else that works. Although ju-jitsu is undoubtedly very effective indeed as an aid to self-defence, some discretion is needed in teaching it to children, as its very effectiveness can make its use dangerous in inappropriate circumstances. Probably most suitable for children from around ten years upwards.

Judo

This is familiar to most people as an Olympic sport, and not really considered a martial art by purists. Judo was developed from ju-jitsu in the late 1800s by the removal of the more potentially dangerous techniques, and the addition of a complicated system of rules and scoring designed to ensure the safety of the competitors. Modern judo is based upon throwing and holding techniques, with chokes, strangles and armlocks allowed only for adult competitors, and is equally suitable for boys and girls. Most clubs will accept children from six to seven years upwards.

Karate

Karate concentrates on striking and kicking techniques, although some styles incorporate a few throws. Karate classes tend to be very disciplined, which can be difficult for younger children to handle. It is suitable for children of eight years upwards.

Kung-fu

Kung-fu is a Chinese martial art very similar to karate, made popular by the films of Bruce Lee. It is based upon striking and kicking techniques, with a large number of different styles and approaches. It is suitable for children over eight.

Kickboxing (or Thai Boxing)

Widely considered to be the most dangerous of the martial arts, this competitive sport allows kicks and punches to the head and legs, both potentially extremely damaging. It is unsuitable for children of any age.

Tae kwon do

This is a form of karate originating from Korea, consisting mainly of punching, kicking and blocking techniques, and characterized by its spectacular jumping and spinning kicks. It is suitable for children from about eight years upwards.

Aikido

Another Japanese art with its roots in ju-jitsu, aikido is non-competitive, and based upon the principles of harmony and non-resistance. Aikido techniques are based on circular movement, and it is one of the few arts in which size and strength have little or no impact on the effectiveness of a technique. Classes tend to be highly disciplined and quite formal. It is suitable for children from eight years upwards.

Kendo/Iaido

Iaido is the art of Japanese swordmanship, while kendo is its sporting equivalent, using a split bamboo sword or *shinai*. Iaido is extremely formal, involving the repeated practise of set sequences of sword techniques, while kendo involves energetic and noisy contests between two *shinai*-wielding contestants, wearing armour to protect them from injury – plenty of opportunity for releasing aggression here. Both are increasing in popularity, and some clubs will accept children. The equipment required is expensive, but may be available on loan from some clubs. Both are suitable for children from about ten years upwards.

Ninjutsu

The Ninja were Japanese warriors for hire as assassins, spies and terrorists, known for their skill in martial arts, and particularly for their use of unusual weapons: throwing stars, smoke bombs, brass knuckles and the like. The term ninjutsu is now widely used to cover a multitude of variations on the martial arts theme, often fairly standard ju-jitsu with a few bits and pieces thrown in for glamour. There is no established and nationally recognized governing body for ninjitsu, and each club should be carefully judged on its own merits. If in doubt, avoid this one.

General points about martial arts

- Any discipline which involves throwing or take-down techniques should be practised on a proper judo or gymnastics mat, which should be in good condition, sufficiently dense to offer protection from a heavy throw, and without gaps or holes.

- Overcrowding in a martial arts class is dangerous. Each member of the class should have sufficient room to practise the techniques he is taught without danger of falling on someone else, off the mat or into any projection or obstacle.

- Instructors should be qualified within their discipline, preferably with a teaching qualification rather than just a black belt or its equivalent, and there should be enough instructors and assistants to properly supervise and help the number of pupils in the class.

- Classes should be divided by age and size. It is not appropriate for younger children to practise with adults (except where the adult is an instructor or assistant), although teenagers are sometimes moved up into adult classes as their ability increases. Sparring or contest between adults and children, or children of widely varying age and size, should not be allowed.

- Punching and kicking, particularly the sort of practice where the pupil strikes out at the air without a target (empty punching/kicking), can damage young joints, which are not fully formed until around twelve years of age, and should be practised only with discretion.

- Discipline is important in any potentially dangerous sport, but classes for children should have a happy atmosphere and be punctuated with games.

If you are considering sending your child to a martial arts class, don't assume that it's a good one just because it takes place in a big sports centre, or because the instructor has an impressive list of competition wins to her name. It takes a special sort of person to teach children, and an impressive competitive record won't tell you anything about the individual's teaching ability. The best way to find out about the club you are interested in is to go along and watch a whole class, and try to talk to other parents and children about their experiences at the club. The instructor should be approachable, and the pupils should not be afraid of her – neither should the parents!

Self-defence

Useful though they may be in building confidence, martial arts classes are unlikely to teach much about avoiding dangerous situations, or handling them in a non-physical way. If you want your child to learn about both physical and non-physical ways out of trouble, a self-defence class is what you need. A good self-defence instructor will cover avoidance, awareness and both physical and non-physical techniques for handling aggression, but is unlikely to accept children under twelve or thirteen years of age, and even then will probably restrict participation to girls and women. There are few self-defence classes catering specifically for children, and doing it very well, but some are just martial arts classes in disguise. The main emphasis of a self-defence class should always be on awareness and avoidance.

If you are lucky enough to find a class in your area that caters for younger people, there are several points to look out for:

- A good self-defence instructor will teach awareness and avoidance of dangerous situations as a first priority, and the use of physical techniques only as a last resort.

- The course should include the relationship between the law and self-defence. Only 'reasonable force' may be used in repelling an attack, any more may result in a court appearance for the victim, while the attacker gets off scot-free!

- Many people need considerable help with confidence-buildng before they can believe themselves capable of self-defence at all, and a good instructor will take this into account, allowing time for group discussion of his pupils' fears and limitations.

- The techniques taught should be practical for a person of average, or less than average, size, strength and fitness, dressed in ordinary street clothes.

- A range of defences should be taught to fit the seriousness of the situation. For example, it may be appropriate to administer a painful blow to the nose or groin of someone bigger than yourself who has you cornered in a dark alley, but you would certainly not be justified in doing the same to someone who was calling you names in a crowded school playground.

- Sessions should be fun! The good instructor knows that everyone learns better when relaxed, and will not take himself so seriously that a good giggle is out of the question.

- Self-defence and martial arts are not the same thing, although many self-defence instructors are simply martial arts instructors teaching the same techniques in a tracksuit. Most martial arts are designed to be used against someone who is playing by the same rules, and rely on techniques which take many years of diligent practise to make really effective. Whilst they can help to build confidence, they will not fulfil an immediate need for the quickest and most effective way out of a threatening situation.

- Members of a self-defence class should not be expected to practise sparring (free fighting) with other pupils or instructors as part of a self-defence training programme. Sparring is of little practical use unless practised as part of an ongoing martial arts course, and can lead to injury. In a real attack, if your first response fails you are in very serious trouble. The last thing you want is to enter into a brawl that you are almost sure to lose.

- Self-defence classes involve the risk of falling, and suitable mats should always be provided (see the section on martial arts earlier in this chapter).

- Self-defence pupils are sometimes expected to buy special suits, badges, T-shirts and membership of an organization. These are of no practical use in self-defence terms, but are a great way of relieving pupils and their parents of hard-earned cash – buying them should be matter of choice.

Well-taught self-defence can be valuable and fun, and perhaps its biggest benefit is that it can help to build confidence. There is a danger of over-confidence, however, and it is important that parents reinforce the instructor's advice on avoidance.

Self-defence and the law

Anyone who is attacked physically may, by law, use 'reasonable force' to nullify the attack. This means that she may hurt the attacker enough to stop his attack and prevent him from attacking further, but may not injure him any more than was necessary to achieve this result.

In theory at least, if the target of an attack uses more than 'reasonable force' against his attacker, he could, depending on his age (see chapter 8) end up in court on assault charges. Where bullying is concerned, however, the target of an attack will usually be either younger, smaller or weaker than his attacker, or will be outnumbered – bullies usually prefer to have the odds stacked in their favour – and unless he has, for instance, used a weapon against an unarmed attacker or caused injuries that are way out of line with the seriousness of the attack or threat, the chances of the police taking any action against him are probably fairly remote. Keeping a record of bullying incidents, in the form of a diary and copies of all correspondence, could prove particularly useful if you were called upon by the police to provide proof that bullying had taken place.

Weapons

The child who knows or fears that she is going to be attacked by bullies may be tempted to carry a weapon in order to defend herself against them. The law regarding weapons is straightforward – it is an offence to carry anything at all which is intended for use as a weapon. A knife or sharpened comb, for instance, have no legitimate use, and the police could confiscate them, and bring charges against a child of ten or over. Using them would almost certainly result in prosecution. Apart from the illegality of carrying a weapon, there is always the danger that an attacker will take it from his victim and use it against him. Carrying a weapon could escalate the violence of the attack, or turn a threat into a physical assault, and children should be strongly advised against arming themselves, and helped to find other ways of tackling the situation and avoiding danger.

There are perfectly innocent items, normally carried around by children, which can be used as 'weapons of convenience' in an emergency: pens, rulers, keys, even rolled-up magazines, and a good self-defence class or book will suggest ways of using them to good effect, should the need arise.

Martial arts and self-defence

As we have seen, martial arts are not particularly useful in a self-defence context. It takes a very long time to become proficient in any martial art, and many are only really effective against someone who attacks you in the 'right' way. A self-defence class will teach a few simple and practical physical techniques, and back them up with lots of advice on avoiding trouble and using non-physical ways out of dangerous situations.

Unfortunately, the general public, and to some extent the law, tends to see everyone who has ever attended a martial arts class as a martial arts 'expert', and this can actually weigh against the victim of an attack who fights back and, in doing so, injures his attacker. The theory is that martial arts training gives an unfair advantage to the 'expert', so that using martial arts knowledge against someone with no such training is the equivalent of using a weapon against an unarmed person. In most cases this is absolute nonsense, and is unlikely to be applied to the younger child, but it is something that anyone who practises martial arts, particularly older children and teenagers, needs to be aware of.

Using skills appropriately

The techniques that children are taught will, in a good martial arts club or self-defence class, be carefully chosen to be safe for them to practise under supervision, but there is still a danger that they will try to demonstrate to their friends in unsuitable circumstances, and cause an accident. A good instructor will be careful to explain to her class that the techniques she teaches are absolutely not to be used outside the club. If your child is learning a martial art or self-defence, you can reinforce the instructor's warning yourself, and tell your child that he will not be allowed to go to classes any more if he misuses his knowledge. He may well respond to this by saying: 'But what if someone attacks me?' Probably the best approach is to say that if he is in real danger, and believes that he is going to be hurt badly or taken somewhere against his will, then it is all right to do anything that he has to do in order to keep safe, but do make it quite clear that this applies only to really exceptional circumstances, and not to playground fights or arguments with friends.

Useful addresses

Youth Access
Magazine Business Centre
11 Newarke Street
Leicester LE1 5SS
Telephone: 01162 558763
A young people's counselling agency which will be able to put you in touch with counsellors in your area.

Childline
Telephone: 0800 1111 (freephone)
A telephone counselling service for children under eighteen with problems of any kind. Childline counsellors will often be able to refer children to local sources of help.

Anti-Bullying Campaign (ABC)
10 Borough High Street
London SE1 9QQ
Telephone: 0171 378 1446
A support group for the parents of children who are being bullied at school. Offers a listening and practical advice service to parents and children. Factsheet available for £1 plus A4 s.a.e.

Exploring Parenthood
Latimer Education Centre
194 Freston Road
London W10 6TT
Telephone: 0181 960 1678
Telephone helpline and free leaflets on a range of subjects, including school bullying. Send s.a.e. for publications list, or ask for information over the telephone. Also runs workshops for parents exploring the issues of parenthood.

Children's Legal Centre
20 Compton Terrace
London N1 2UN
Telephone: 0171 359 6251

Aims to represent the interests of children and young people in all matters of law and policy affecting them. Advice on legal matters relating to children.

Childwatch
206 Hessle Road
Hull
N. Humberside HU3 3BE
Telephone: 01482 25552
Advice on protection, prevention and coping with bullying, both at school and within the family. Telephone and face-to-face counselling for adults suffering from the after-effects of childhood abuse. Send £1.50 (including p. & p.) for their child protection pack, or ring for advice.

Parent Network
Telephone: 0171 485 8535
A national network of local parent support groups, helping parents and children to feel better about themselves and each other and handle the ups and downs of family life.

Parentline
Telephone: 01268 757077
A network of parent-run groups offering telephone listening and support to parents under stress. Will often be able to provide details of other local sources of help. Ring this number for details of your local group.

Victim Support
Cranmer House
39 Brixton Road
London SW9 6DZ
Telephone: 0171 735 9166
A national network of local victim support schemes, offering a mixture of emotional support, practical advice and information. Victim Support has conducted extensive research into the effects on children of crime, including bullying, and aims to have specialist workers in most areas within two years. Most referrals come from the police, but individuals are welcome to make contact themselves. Children under seventeen will be seen with their parents' consent.

Kidscape
152 Buckingham Palace Road
London SW1W 9TR
Telephone: 0171 730 3300
A charity devoted to the protection and safety of children. Kidscape
has developed a variety of practical, positive programmes to teach
children how to cope with bullying, stranger danger, danger from
known adults, etc., and provides training and resources for teachers
and other professionals. Send a large s.a.e. for free leaflets and
details of books and videos.

The Sports Council
16 Upper Woburn Place
London WC1H 0QP
Telephone: 0171 388 1277
National headquarters will put you in touch with your regional HQ
for information about sports available in your area. May also have
details of self-defence classes.

National Association of Youth Theatres
Unit 1304
The Custard Factory
Gibb Street
Digbeth
Birmingham B9 4AA
Telephone: 0121 608 2111
Send a s.a.e. for details of drama groups in your area.

Education Otherwise
36 Kinross Road
Leamington Spa
Warwickshire CV32 7EF
Telephone: 01926 886828
Support group for home-educating families.

The Children's Home-Based Education Association
14 Basil Avenue
Armthorpe
Doncaster DN3 2AT
Telephone: 01302 833596
Supports home education.

111

Further reading

Family life

Baker, Carol, *Getting on with Your Children*. Longman 1990.
Crabtree, Tom, *A-Z of Children's Emotional Problems*. Unwin 1984.
Jaques, Penny, *Understanding Children's Problems*. Unwin 1987. Readable and practical insights into understanding and coping with the ups and downs of family life.

Bullying, for parents

Elliot, Michele, *A Practial Guide to Talking with Children*. Hodder & Stoughton 1988. Helping your child to develop strategies for dealing with potentially dangerous situations.
Pearce, Dr John, *Fighting, Teasing and Bullying*. Thorsons 1989. Simple and effective ways to help your child handle their own and others' aggression.

Bullying, for children

Elliott, Michele, *Willow Street Kids*. Deutsch/Pan 1986, 1992 (new ed.) Fictional stories about a group of children and how they deal with bullying, strangers and so on. Commonsense, practical advice for children of seven to eleven years old.
Elliott, Michele, *Bullies Meet the Willow Street Kids*. Pan Macmillan 1993. Sequel to the *Willow Street Kids*, in which they meet and deal with a gang of bullies. For children of seven to eleven years old.
Elliott, Michele, *Feeling Happy, Feeling Safe*. Hodder 1991. Colourful story-book with positive safety messages for children of two to six years old. Available from Kidscape.

Bullying, for Schools

Elliott, Michele (ed.). *Bullying: A Practical Guide to Coping For Schools*. Longman 1991.

Index